Matthew Byrne

D1622153

The Way It Was

THE NARRATIVE OF THE BIRTH OF JESUS

the columba press

First published in 2004 by
the columba press
55A Spruce Avenue, Stillorgan Industrial Park,
Blackrock, Co Dublin

Cover by Bill Bolger
Origination by The Columba Press
Printed in Ireland by ColourBooks Ltd, Dublin

ISBN 1 85607 463 3

Acknowledgements
The biblical text used is the version from *Luke: A Greek-English Diglot for the use of Translators*, published by The British and Foreign Bible Society, 1962. Used by kind permission.

The birth of Christ was like this …
St Matthew 1:18

In memory
of
my parents
Elizabeth and Patrick
whom I loved
and who loved me
and showed me
a good path to walk along

Table of Contents

Preface

St Matthew and St Luke write about the birth of Jesus and each of them presents his own 'exclusive cover' of the event. Which is not surprising. Every reporter brings his own style and colour to the piece he writes. The evangelists are no different.

St Matthew's account is crisp, tight. He writes no more than the salient details, the bare essentials for the record he presents.

It's his method, shaped by years of book-keeping as a tax-collector, a *publicanus*. He spent a lifetime in his tax-collector's booth, registering what was paid, and making concise, succinct notes of those who paid, those who didn't and were given a threat, and those who had defaulted long enough to warrant a spell in jail till the debt was paid.

St Luke is the physician. Sensitive, observant, sympathetic. He can't help feeling the human emotion of things. And he writes in language that expresses it.

The Way It Was is a look of the evangelists' account, to light up the background of what they've written, and to try to see more closely the personalities they glance at, and who play so large a part in the events surrounding the birth.

It's no more than an attempt at an exposition of the familiar gospel text we hold in our hands. In the hope of feeling a way through the mists and notions that cloud the evangelists' record, to see the birth the way it was. And, in the process, see more clearly the movement of the hand of God in the history of nations, and the affairs of ordinary mortals.

I am indebted to my late and good friend Dr Eric T. Holden. In days long gone, he introduced me to *Tropical Medicine* by Rogers and Megaw when I was researching Herod's illness. I owe a debt, too, to the late, and lamented, Professor F. F. Bruce. He was my supervisor when I was a research student at Manchester. A patient man he was, who shared liberally of his wisdom and scholarship.

I thank the Reverend Olivia H. Williams. She read the script as it was being written. Her criticism was kind, but to the point; her advice generous and well-informed.

CHAPTER ONE

Introduction

Jesus of Nazareth is, on any count, an important figure in history.

Categorising him, however, in order to compare him with some other outstanding world personality, is difficult. Once you begin to try, the list of his achievements grows till it starts to look like the old 'tinker, tailor' rhyme – thinker, teacher, healer, preacher, wit, raconteur, politician, controversialist, religionist, historian, theologian, messiah …

He has to rank amongst the leading philosophers of the world. His philosophy is expounded simply and explicitly in the famous Sermon on the Mount. It is, and has been for almost two thousand years, the basis of a worldwide way of life, eagerly accepted by some, held in contempt by others, and stubbornly debated by all, lived in love and serenity, fought over and died for.

As a teacher, Jesus seemed able to establish immediate rapport with his audience. He had a facility for taking the ordinary concerns and interests of everyday life, and turning them into vehicles that conveyed to ordinary people the deep things of his teaching. Yet he never laid down hard and fast rules. He seems to have preferred establishing great principles. Not the least of his characteristics as a teacher was the fact that he not only taught the virtue of love, he lived it. His life was the centre and illustration of his teaching.

He was an unashamed entertainer. And while no part of his life history records that he ever smiled, let alone laughed, there is enough to suggest that he enjoyed the laughter of others, for example, the parable of the friend at midnight or the illustration of the camel going through the eye of a needle, which are enough to make anybody laugh.

That his laughter has no mention in the record does not mean that he knew nothing of true human emotion. He knew it all, anger, grief, love, wonder, joy, sighing, sorrow and weeping.

His humour, however, was part of the stock-in-trade of his preacher's art. He had also sarcasm and subtle innuendo. He could be vitriolic when the occasion demanded, and loosed his invective on individuals and groups alike.

As a controversialist he was a master. At times he allowed his opponents to grind their own arguments into the ground. At others he cut the legs from under them with cold logic. And there were occasions when he found it hard to suffer fools gladly, even when they were numbered amongst his own close followers.

In the field of literature he has few equals. His short story of the 'Prodigal Son,' is accepted as the perfect short story.

His life is marked by an almost obsessive religious devotion. The enthusiasm that characterised his childhood, appears in adulthood as a rounded, well-versed, well-educated grasp of the literature, theology, history and tradition of his religion. His loyalty to the religion of his nation often enough brought him into conflict with its guardians, whom he considered neglectful in their care of it, where they were not blatently misrepresenting it, and abusing their position of authority.

From the emphasis put on Jesus's work as a healer, it would be easy to gain the impression that he spent every waking moment healing the sick. That he healed people is beyond question. It was, however, only part of his mission. A fundamental and inevitable part, indeed, but a part that must be kept in careful perspective, as the New Testament writers suggest by offering a total of only twenty-five healings by Jesus, with a few mentions of the healing missions he conducted.

At the same time, though, it ought to be borne in mind that Jesus did not consider his being a healer as marking him as unique. He himself recognised, and reminded others that healing the sick was a ministry already long established and practised in Israel.

Jesus arrived on the scene when Israel's political expectations and ambitions were smouldering dangerously.

As a boy he cannot fail to have known of the rebellion led by Judas the Galilean, and heard the battle-cry of the gangs he headed in insurrection against Rome's assuming direct government in Judaea and Samaria – 'We have no Lord and Master but God.'

The nation still smarted from Judas's defeat, and its fermenting hate of the conqueror was carefully nurtured by the political party known as the Zealots.

Jesus finished his last days on earth in the same prison as Barabbas, a popular participant in yet another insurrection.

Between the two – Judas and Barabbas – there were countless unnamed individuals who set themselves up as messiahs in Israel, and kept alive the Jewish confidence that Rome's eventual defeat by a Jewish army, under a Bethlehem-born messiah, at Arbela, to the west of the Sea of Galilee. Jewish legend called it Armageddon.

Jesus made no bones about his being, not just a messiah, but The Messiah in Israel. All other claimants he contemptuously dismissed as 'false messiahs'.

He so obviously had the makings of a national political leader. He had the charisma of the greatest of the Old Testament heroes and prophets. His grip on the ordinary people, and his effortless success in exciting them, disturbed those in authority in Israel who viewed him as a constant threat to the uneasy balance they had managed to manipulate for the nation with conquering Rome.

Had he been so minded, he might have been made king by popular acclaim. As it was, however, Jesus set himself to disabuse his followers of the messianic ideas they harboured, arguing the wrongness of their conception of things. His messiahship did not mean the redemption of Israel through an all-out military conquest. The messiahship for Jesus meant setting men free through his own death. It was a truth which hardly dawned on his followers during his lifetime, and took long enough to dawn even after he had endured the death he had prophesied for himself.

The evangelists were the first to make any serious attempt at 'publishing' any kind of record of the life and work of Jesus.

Their finished product, on the face of it, looks like the biography of any other historical figure – beginning at the birth, and finishing with the completion of his life's work.

A slightly closer look, though, reveals that these writers use up most of their space in recording his death. Indeed, it is this interest in his death that motivates them into making the record in the first place. And while they appear to deal with his life in some sort of chronological order, they are, in fact, writing with hindsight, and an agenda.

Their whole approach to the record is coloured by the significance they attach to his death. And more than that, they write with the conviction that he is risen from the dead.

This resurrection is important for them, for, so far as they judge it, the resurrection gives meaning to the death of Jesus, and is a seal that what he came to do, he accomplished. If he came as God in the flesh to 'give his life a ransom for many,' the resurrection is proof of the reality of his work.

So that while the evangelists appear to begin at the beginning, they are really working back. Even their record of his birth is presented with the conviction that Jesus was the supernatural being making an entry as mortal man amongst mortal men – 'God hath visited his people.' This is for them the basic reason for writing of the birth of Jesus Christ.

St Matthew and St Luke had no idea, when they wrote about the birth of Jesus of Nazareth, that their account would still be being read two thousand years later. Had they had the slightest inkling, it is fairly certain they'd have done things differently.

What they did was fine in the circumstances, when it's remembered they were writing for the people of their own day. For people who were aware of the customs and prejudices and attitudes of the time. For people who breathed the spiritual and religious atmosphere of the day, and could appreciate angels and visions and dreams, and the prevailing hope that Messiah would come.

Because they were living in a land where little changed over the long years, they would be familiar with the matters the evangelists wrote of – betrothal, marriage, divorce, the social and religious customs attached to pregnancy and childbirth.

This familiarity meant that they did not need everything spelled-out in fine detail.

In these circumstances, the evangelists could naturally assume that their readers would see the account against a familiar backdrop. What was already so much part and parcel of their way of life as to be part of their subconscious would, almost automatically, fill in the background.

St Matthew and St Luke could afford, then, to write their account briefly. In shorthand, almost.

As the years passed, however, and the church spread beyond Palestine and the Jewish environment. Christians could no longer be expected to have so intimate and easy an understanding of the background.

It was inevitable that later Christians should try to enhance what the evangelists had written briefly, filling in the gaps in their knowledge, and answering the questions of their minds with the pious fictions of their imagination.

The unhappy result of their pious, well-intentioned efforts make God look like a master magician, and Jesus something of a boy-wonder.

The process was well established by the middle of the second century. And the next six hundred years saw the appearance of documents like *A Gospel of the Infancy, The history of Joseph the Carpenter, A Gospel of the Infancy of Blessed Mary*.

These writings later gained the title Apocryphal Gospels. They never became part of the canonical New Testament. They disappeared from circulation for centuries, but came into vogue again in Europe in the Middle Ages.

The poets and ballad-makers of those times used them as the bases for their literary works. The painters and artists of the age gave lasting substance to the legends in their works of art.

The results appealed to pious, uncritical minds, but, in reality, had little or no obvious warrant in the New Testament.

The effect of all this was that the views and sentiments of

these Apocryphal Gospels had enormous influence on the reading and interpretation of the New Testament record of the birth
of Jesus. So enormous, in fact, that when the New Testament
was translated into English, the presentation of the birth narrative was coloured by the outlook of these Apocryphal Gospels.

And the influence has hardly lessened over the centuries. It is
so strong, even today, that interpretations are foisted on the
evangelists' account that are hard to support from the text.

For the most part, we have adapted the narrative of the birth
of Jesus to suit our taste. We have turned the record into a folk
tale, littered with sacred cows which are so much part of our
traditional Christmas scene, that any attempt at contradicting
them looks like a threat to fundamental truth.

The fact that the traditional tale finds no support in the
evangelists' original hardly seems to matter. Indeed, it is woe
betide anybody who dares to tamper with what is solemnly misunderstood from the time we could first remember. And had
our misconceptions reinforced by 'Once in royal David's city,'
'Away in a manger,' 'We three kings of Orient are,' and a host of
other carols which, while beautifully sentimental, misrepresent
the evangelists' history of the event.

Books are still written as though their authors were unaware
that they are purveying the myth more than the truth. And
every year countless nativity plays re-enact and reinforce the
apocryphal stories so pausibly that young, unformed minds are
grossly ill-informed. And even older, otherwise critical, minds
are dulled into accepting the fiction for the fact.

Pious imagination is one thing. Pious fiction is another. Pious
imagination can help us grasp something of the miracle in the
event. Pious fiction degrades the miraculous, and smothers the
uniqueness of the happening in a froth of sentimentality. And it
makes a nonsense of the care St Matthew and St Luke took in
presenting the record in the first place.

St Matthew and St Luke are the only gospel writers who deal
with the birth of Jesus in any detail.

St Mark and St John do not mention it. This does not mean, though, that they were not aware of it or did not appreciate the special circumstances that surrounded it. If they do not spell out the intimate details, it is because they are not necessary to their presentation of the ministry of Jesus.

St Mark bursts into his presentation of things with 'The beginning of the gospel of Jesus Christ, the Son of God.' And then, with the breathless economy of a man who would tell everything all at once, he bounds along, retailing episodes from the ministry of Jesus, with the single purpose of leading his readers to the conviction that Jesus, on earth, was the Son of God. The Incarnation.

But he knows about the birth. And he knows that Jesus's listeners knew about the birth. But for them there was nothing of the miraculous in it. It was, as they reckoned, more the frailty of human nature, and 'the ways of a man with a maid.' Is not this 'the son of Mary?' they jibed when they were rejecting him for the second time in Nazareth. And they meant it offensively because, as St Mark explains, 'they were offended at him'.

St John declares his conviction about Jesus in the banner headline to his gospel – 'The Word was made flesh, and dwelt among us.'

He cannot have been unaware of the peculiar circumstances of Jesus's birth. He was, after all, his cousin, son of Salome, the Virgin Mary's younger sister.

He uniquely records two intimate episodes involving the mother of Jesus and her son.

The first, the marriage at Cana. He reports a conversation between Jesus and his mother that is reminiscent of their conversation during their visit to the Temple in his early boyhood. The second episode was at Calvary, when St John allows us to overhear the concern of a devoted son for his mother who was about to be bereaved.

At the same time, though, he gives clues that the people of our Lord's day had their own view of his birth. It was no 'God taking flesh,' no incarnation for them. They saw no more than the human circumstances of the event. And were not beyond using it as a jibe against him when he asserted his divinity and assumed the divine name.

'We were not born of fornication,' is their comment, as St John records it, affording evidence that they were aware enough of the human circumstances surrounding his birth for the barb to be designed to insult and hurt him.

St Matthew and St Luke take pains with their account of the nativity, conscious of the significance of the events they report ... St Matthew aware of the relevance of the birth of Jesus to the Jewish people, St Luke alert to its place in world history, and its meaning to all mankind.

Their record, then, is not just the story of the birth of a man named Jesus who ultimately earned the title, 'The Son of God.' This is the record of the Incarnation, God coming in flesh amongst men.

With a simplicity that might be misconstrued, both St Matthew and St Luke spell out the intimate details of the act of Incarnation. They bring us as close to the physical scene as human eye, mind and emotion can approach.

St Matthew does it because, for him, the birth of Jesus Christ, like every other detail of the life, death and resurrection of Jesus, is the sum, summary and consummation of Old Testament prophecy. St Luke does it because having, as he says himself, 'gone over the whole course of these events in detail,' he commits himself to giving his readers 'a connected narrative ... authentic knowledge of the matters about which you have been informed.'

Their painstaking efforts give us, not a homespun tale to be interpreted as whim and fancy and novelty might dictate. But rather a narrative of the Incarnation to be read and marked with no less care, that we might catch some sight of the Supernatural breaking into time and the affairs of mortal men.

CHAPTER TWO

Zacharias
St Luke 1:5-25

I thought it good, as I have been thoroughly familiar with everything from the beginning, to write it down in proper order ...

St Luke sets his own standard, and states his plan and purpose clearly – to present things in order. And he starts as he means to go on.

In the record of the birth of Jesus, the angelic visitor will recommend that Mary consider her cousin Elizabeth, a woman well-beyond child-bearing age, who is now, in fact, six months pregnant.

The reader must not be put in the position of having to guess the what and the why of Elizabeth's pregnancy.

St Luke, therefore, introduces his account of the birth of Jesus with a review of how matters stand with Mary's cousin. It is, though, no mere preface to St Luke's birth narrative. It is an essential and significant part of it. And the time and care St Luke takes in relating it, suggests his awareness of its importance.

He is writing about the birth of John the Baptist, the fore-runner of Jesus in every sense of the word.

The Baptist is born before Jesus. He prepares the way for Jesus. He baptises him. He identifies Jesus as 'the Lamb of God,' and announces his mission and ministry – 'to take away the sin of the world.'

In the days of Herod, king of Judaea, there was a priest named Zacharias, belonging to Abijah's division. His wife was a descendant of Aaron; her name was Elizabeth. Both were law-abiding in God's eyes, going in all the commandments and requirements of the Lord blamelessly. But they were childless because Elizabeth was barren, and both were advanced in years.

19

A gentle priest and his no less gentle wife – both well-advanced in years – made history unawares. And St Luke writes them into the history books. 'In the days of Herod the king, there was a priest …'

St Luke makes the note that Elizabeth was 'of the daughters of Aaron'. In saying so, he makes it clear she was a fit woman to be married to a priest. A priest might marry a virgin or a widow, but not a woman who was divorced. She must be of the same nation. And, before marrying her, he must (according to the Jewish historian, Josephus) 'make a scrutiny, and take his wife's genealogy from the ancient tables, and procure many witnesses to it.'

'Both,' says St Luke, 'were law-abiding in God's eyes, going in all the commandments of the Lord blamelessly.'

This is not a character reference. It is more by way of explaining that if, in fact, they had no children, it was through no fault of their own. Zacharias and Elizabeth lived in a day when it was considered that, if a couple were childless, it was because they were guilty of some unknown, unconfessed and unforgiven sin. It was a punishment from God.

This, however, was not the case with the priest and his wife, as St Luke explains. The sad truth was that Elizabeth could not conceive a child. 'Elizabeth was barren.'

Did any of those in the community, who could so readily condemn and scorn, ever stop to imagine the stress and anxiety Elizabeth and Zacharias endured? Or wonder about the heartache of having their hope dashed month after month, year after saddening year? Or even how much, how often in their frustration they entreated God to bless them with a child? Till the time came when there was neither cause nor reason anymore for them to hope. Zacharias was an old man, and his wife was, as the priest, with the tender elegance of a gentleman still in love, describes her, 'advanced in years.'

Zacharias is introduced as being about his daily duties as a priest in the Temple.

He is a member of one of the twenty-four divisions or courses of priests who serve in the Temple.

There were something like one thousand priests in each division, living in thirteen towns conveniently adjacent to Jerusalem and the Temple. The divisions worked on a rota basis that went back to the time of king David.

Zacharias belonged to the Eighth division which was known as Abijah's division.

Each priest served his duty a week at a time – from one Sabbath to the next. And while on duty, he lived in a room in the cloisters of the Outer Court of the Temple.

It fell to Zacharias's lot, as part of his duty, that on one of the days he would make the incense offering. This is the occasion St Luke writes about.

While he was on priestly duty in God's presence
in the turn of his division according to the custom
of the priesthood, it fell to him by lot
to enter the sanctuary of the Lord
and make the incense-offering.
The whole community of the people
were praying outside
at the hour of the incense-offering.
An angel of the Lord appeared to him,
standing on the right of the altar of incense.
Zacharias was troubled when he saw him,
and fear seized him.
The angel said to him, 'Do not be afraid, Zacharias;
your prayer has been heard.
Your wife Elizabeth will bear you a son,
and you shall name him John;
you will have joy and delight,
and many will rejoice at his birth.
For he will be great in the eyes of the Lord,
he will drink no wine or strong drink,
he will be filled with the Holy Spirit,
right from his mother's womb,
and he will turn many of the Israelites to the Lord their God.
He will go forward in his sight in the spirit and power

of Elijah, to turn the minds of fathers to their children,
and convert the disobedient by the wisdom of the righteous,
to make ready for the Lord a people thoroughly prepared.'

Zacharias said to the angel, 'By what shall I know this?
I am an old man and my wife is advanced in years.'

The angel answered him, 'I am Gabriel,
he who stands before God.
I have been sent to speak to you and give you this good news.
Mark this, you will be silent, unable to speak,
until the day when this happens
because you did not believe my words,
which shall be fulfilled at their appointed time.'

The people were expecting Zacharias
and were astonished that he was so long in the sanctuary.

When he came out he could not speak to them,
and they realised he had seen a vision in the sanctuary.
He kept making signs to them,
and he remained dumb.

Then when the days of his service were completed,
he returned home.

St Luke's note is brief and concise. And looks lopsided, with all
the emphasis on the angel and the angel's message. Under-
standably. His main concern is to establish the announcement
from heaven of the birth of a son to Zacharias the priest, the son
who will be John the Baptist.

It would be easy to read the record and see Zacharias as the
recipient who, having recovered from his initial fright and
shock, hears and accepts the message with equanimity. It is only
at the end of the announcement that he speaks, presuming – in
view of the fact that 'I am an old man ...' – to ask the question,
'How can I be sure of this?' The question, though, and the messenger's response hint that there was a great deal more going on
in Zacharias's mind than a casual reading might suggest.

Zacharias's question is not something which suddenly

springs into his mind. It has to be the result of an attitude which has been building up from the very start of the heavenly visitor's announcement. What he could not understand, he found difficult to believe.

The situation becomes clearer if we feel our way through the episode, trying to see things from the old priest's point of view.

Making the morning Incense Offering was considered a very great privilege. The offering was made on a special altar in the Holy Place, separated only by a veil from the Holy of Holies, the place of the abiding Presence of the Almighty.

The task of making the offering, then, brought the priest nearer the Presence of God than any other priestly act in the Temple, and carried with it the promise of receiving the richest blessings of heaven. For this reason, which priest would officiate was decided by lot.

Even without that rule, though, it's hard to imagine how he might have done it more often. A priest did duty in the Temple for only two separate weeks in the year. He was a member of a division of about a thousand priests. In the circumstances, then, the possibility of making the Incense Offering more than once would seem remote in the extreme. That the rule existed at all is an indication of the great privilege and high dignity associated with the act.

Zacharias is standing in the Court of the Priests.

Behind him is the Great Altar of unhewn stone on which, in a few minutes, the morning sacrifice will be offered. Immediately in front of him is the entrance to the Holy Place, its vast, great , gold-panelled doors wide open. On either side of the doors, the walls too are plated with gold. And above them a golden vine from which hang clusters of golden grapes, as long as a man is tall.

Through the gleaming doors, he can see the interior of the Holy Place, its walls glittering with beaten gold. To his right, as he looks – on the north side – is the table of the shew-bread, with its twelve unleavened loaves set six upon six, representing, it was said, the zodiac and the twelve months of the year, and the Twelve Tribes of the Children of Israel. To his left, the golden candlestick of seven branches, its lights burning. The lamps, it was said, represented the seven planets, and a memento of the pillar that had led their forefathers in the long-gone past. Between them, the altar of incense where he would make the morning offering.

He could see – beyond the table, the candlestick and the altar – the vast Babylonian tapestry so richly embroidered with blue and scarlet and white and purple, and as large as the great gold-plated doors it hid and shielded. It was called the Veil of the Temple. It separated the Holy Place from the Holy of Holies, the place of God's abiding Presence, where none entered except the High Priest. And he entered only once a year, on the Day of Atonement.

A ringing bell would signal that the morning sacrifice was about to be laid on the Great Altar. It would also be a signal to Zacharias to enter the Holy Place and make the incense offering.

Zacharias waited, clothed in his white priestly vestments, his head covered with a white turban, his feet naked. He held in his hands the golden vessel of incense. Waiting with him was a companion priest who would assist him. He held a bowl of the glowing embers he had taken from the continually burning fire on the Great Altar.

Exhilaration, elation, fear, awe, delight, apprehension, humility, excitement, fright, honour, anxiety, privilege … Zacharias felt it all, and all at once, in one overwhelming, smothering conglomeration. And all the while, in his head, a bell tingling, tinkling, urging him to move when he could do no more than stand stock still.

A gentle pressure at his elbow eased him forward, and he was standing before the altar of incense.

He was aware of his assisting companion spreading the embers on the altar, fanning them gently into a brighter glow.

His companion, his task completed, withdrew. Backwards, like a courtier leaving the presence of his king.

And Zacharias was alone. A privileged priest in the Holy Place.

By now, he knew, the priests, more alert to the summoning bell than himself, would already be in their appointed places in their Court around the Great Altar of sacrifice. The Levites would be ready to sing, and the trumpeters poised and waiting to sound the time for the morning sacrifice.

The worshippers waited, the men in the Court of the Israelites, ranged round the Sanctuary, the women in theirs. And, far back, beyond the steps and the warning notice that barred their entry into the inner courts, the Gentiles in the Court of the Gentiles.

The murmur-murmur of their prayers had stopped, and in tense, hushed expectancy, every face was turned towards the Holy Place waiting for the cloud to ascend from the incense burning on the altar.

Gently, gently, as though it were a frail thing, Zacharias held the golden bowl, sprinkling incense over the hot coals on the altar, till he saw the first cloud form, shaping itself along the glowing embers.

He was making the incense offering for the first time in his long priesthood. And, he reminded himself, for the last time. Not just because tradition ordained it so, but because, as common sense instructed him, he was too old ever to have another opportunity.

His wife, Elizabeth, would be pleased. And he was looking forward, when the next Sabbath was ended, to getting back home to Juttah in the hill country, to tell her all about it.

The sweet odour of the burning incense was already filling the Holy Place. And it was beautiful, Zacharias thought. A fitting offering to the Lord of the Universe. He sprinkled what remained in the bowl onto the fire, and watched the cloud rise and rise, wreathing its way to fill the Temple, and lift the prayers of the faithful up to heaven.

Now it was time to leave. By now the worshippers would see the smoke of the incense. They would be waiting for him to come out again. Then the trumpets would sound throughout the Temple, and it would be time for the first sacrifice – a male lamb, the first burnt offering of the day.

He turned the incense vessel over, and shook it, to be certain there were no grains left. There was none. Though, he didn't expect any. And might not have noticed even if one or two were to have fallen out. His eye and attention were lost in looking, through the rising smoke, at the tapestry of the Veil behind the altar.

How often he had seen the Veil. All through his boyhood, and all through the years of his priesthood. But always at a distance. Never so close. And, certainly, never so close for so long. He feasted his eyes on it, trying to see everything, every detail. Not just the splendour of its colours, the purple and blue and scarlet and flaxen white – the holy colours of Israel – but the embroidery, the stitches, and how the threads were worked … till it seemed as though it depicted every flower, every plant that grew under the sun.

And human hands, he reminded himself, had made all this. Fingers had bled and grown calloused with the work. Eyes tired. Backs ached. And furrowed, concentrating brows had dropped sweat … but what a work it was …

He took it all in, noting the whorls and the knots and hatchings, the cross-stitching, the twists and turns of threads, the colours, here glaring, boisterous, brazen, there blending, modest, soft and gentle. He would remember every detail, he convinced himself. He would tell his wife all about it as soon as he was home again … Poor Elizabeth … she would get no peace for all his talking.

He made a deep obeisance, and began to move away backwards from the altar. But stopped, suddenly sensing some kind of presence to his right. He could not move to look, but the corner of his eye caught the shape of a figure at the right-hand side of the altar. It was imagination, he assured himself. No man ever stood there. The right side of the altar was the place where nobody ever stood. It was all no more than the shapes and shadows of the incense smoke, he told himself. He was mistaken.

But the more sure he was that he was mistaken, so much the more the awareness of the presence pressed and weighed upon him. Someone, something was there.

Fear and fright slowly turned his head, and made him look.

The figure was there. At the right-hand side of the altar. It had the face and form and the appearance of a man. But it was not a man. It was substantial as a body is substantial, but it was not a body. It cast no shadow, and seemed to make no weight upon the ground it stood on.

Zacharias tried to look away, but his head would not move. He could not avert his eyes. He felt overwhelmed.

But not, now, the awe and wonder, the exhilaration he had known while he made the incense offering. Now it was fear. Taut, tension-tying fear. And guilt. He had, unknowingly, committed some heinous sin in the Holy Place. He had taken too much pleasure in the beauty and slendour of the place. He had neglected the worship of God for the admiration of earthly, man-made things. And even now, he was compounding his offences. For while he tarried so long in the Holy Place, the people must wait, the trumpets could not sound, and the morning sacrifice could not be offered.

This, then, was most surely a visitation from heaven itself, to announce God's punishment for his misdeeds and offences, and afflict him with sore punishment.

He was held in terror's thrall. And, like an animal snared in a gin-trap, he waited for his hunter's killing blow to strike.

His eyes were fixed, locked tight on the form in front of him, hypnotised by the sight, every fibre in his body strung to breaking-point. His feet and legs would not move that he might run from this place, and flee the fright and terror that assailed him. And sweat poured from every pore, cold sweat that chilled and wetted him, and soaked into his priestly robes … even the incense vessel in his hands was wet from his sweat, and he feared that he would let it fall … This was fear he had never known before …

Heaven's messenger spoke. 'Zacharias,' he called out, 'Do not be afraid.'

The priest almost laughed out loud. Not knowing why, but trying to take in and believe that there would be no great condemnation, no punishment.

His fear, though, did not go away. It still gnawed at him. Fear that wracked and terrorised a man could not be dissipated by a mere word as though it were no more than a stray thought idling through the mind. The messenger, Zacharias reminded himself, had come on a mission. There was more to say. And Zacharias still feared.

'Your prayer,' the angel told him, 'your entreaty has been heard ...'

What prayer? the priest wondered. During all the time he had been in the Holy Place, he had offered no prayer ... For long years of his life he had made only one entreaty, and that constantly. But age and God's ordained nature had brought an end to that. And he could not, now, count the years since last he had mouthed the plea to the Maker and Sustainer of the Universe ... And heaven's ears had remained deaf, and his entreaty left unanswered ...

'Your wife Elizabeth will bear a son,' the angel was declaring. It was a cruel thing to say, Zacharias thought, a callous thing. Could God who had sent the messenger be so cruel, so unthinking, without understanding or kindness ... There was nothing else he so often and so fervently wished for Elizabeth. But not now, not now. She was too long past the age of childbearing. The angel's message had come too late. Far, far too late.

But the messenger did not wait. He had a message to deliver whether Zacharias heard it or not, whether the priest understood it or not, whether Zacharias thought it right or not. 'You shall name him John. You will have joy and delight, and many will rejoice at his birth ...'

Zacharias tried not to hear. This was punishment by mockery. Would heaven send a messenger to mock an old man, a man who had kept the commandments, and lived godly all his days ...

'He will be great in the eyes of the Lord. He will drink no wine or strong drink. He will be filled with the Holy Spirit from his mother's womb, and he will turn many of the Israelites to the Lord their God ...'

But Elizabeth, his wife, was barren. She could not conceive a child. She was long beyond bearing a child. What the angel was saying was beyond belief. The experience of life told him it was unnatural. The wisdom of old age said it was impossible. And if the messenger would pause, he would tell him so.

But the angel did not pause. The voice went on and on, delivering the message as though the messenger had learnt it all by rote.

'He will go forward in his sight in the spirit and power of Elijah, to turn the minds of fathers to their children, and convert the disobedient by the wisdom of the righteous, to make ready for the Lord a people thoroughly prepared.'

It is all beyond the old priest's comprehension. And what he cannot understand, he finds difficult to believe. He is shouting back before he realises what he is doing or saying. 'By what shall I know this?' 'How can I be certain of this?' It is not a question so much as a protestation. He cannot believe what he is hearing. It contradicts everything he knows and has experienced. And, for a very good reason. 'I am an old man, and my wife is advanced in years.'

The air is taut with silence. Tension laden. Till the messenger speaks. 'I am Gabriel. He who stands before God.'

Matters might have been different for Zacharias, they would certainly have been easier, had the messenger revealed his identity at the very beginning. Now, with his 'I am Gabriel, he who stands before God,' the messenger is establishing his *bona fides*, his credentials. Even pulling rank! He comes from God's immediate presence. He does God's bidding. He does important business. He is sent to communicate important messages. And Zacharias is only too suddenly aware of it. He knows about angels. Belief in angels has been part of Israelite religion since time immemorial.He knows about Gabriel. But Zacharias gets no opportunity, now, to explain himself or offer any excuse or apology. 'I have been sent to speak to you, and give you this good news …'

Zacharias, even though he could not grasp or understand precisely what it all meant, might have been content, now, to accept what the angel had communicated. And given the chance, he might have said so in so many words. But he was not given the chance. Instead, the angel went on speaking. And warns him, 'Mark this, you will be silent, unable to speak, until the day this happens, because you did not believe my words, which will be fulfilled at their appointed time.'

The visitation was ended. As quickly and quietly as he had come, so the messenger was gone again.

Outside, beyond the Holy Place – in the Court of the Priests, in the Court of the Israelites, the Court of the Women, and the farther Court of the Gentiles – the people waited, expecting Zacharias. They 'were astonished that he was so long in the sanctuary'.

Awe-stricken, shaken by his experience, still smarting from the reprimand, Zacharias left the Holy Place.

He had already delayed the worship and the people too long. He came out of the Sanctuary, and made to tell them what had happened at the Altar of Incense ... But he could not speak ... He was dumb, as the angel had warned him. And he remained dumb for all he tried to speak to the people. He had to resort to making signs to try to explain to them what had occurred.

They drew their own conclusions, deciding that he had seen a vision in the Sanctuary.

His task finished, Zacharias left the Sanctuary. And when his tour of duty was completed, he returned home. Full of important news about significant happenings. But unable to speak of them.

After these days his wife Elizabeth conceived,
and she hid herself for five months,
saying 'This is what the Lord has done for me
at the time when he looked on me
to take away my reproach among men.'

St Luke will, later on in his account, write about the birth of the son the angel had spoken of.

In the meantime, he ends this part of the history of things by stating that 'Elizabeth conceived. And she hid herself ...'

The 'hiding' had nothing to do with modesty or even embar-
rassment at having conceived a child in her advanced years.
Indeed, Elizabeth seems to have been quite pleased with herself,
happy in the feeling that God had turned his attention to her,
and had specially blessed her. 'This is what the Lord has done
for me ...' she declares, 'to take away my reproach ...'

The expression St Luke uses to describe what Elizabeth did
means 'she kept herself at home,' (*periekruben eauten*). In the circumstances, it seems an eminently sensible course to follow.

Elizabeth cossetted and cared for herself, taking wise and
proper precautions in the early and uneasy days of her pregnancy.
A younger woman might have been confident and comfortable
about her forming baby after the first three months of pregnancy.
Elizabeth, not only an older woman, but beyond the normal age
for bearing a child, was extra cautious and vigilant. And 'kept
herself at home'.

CHAPTER THREE

The Annunciation
St Luke 1:26-38

*In the sixth month the angel Gabriel was sent from God
to a city of Galilee named Nazareth,
to a maiden betrothed to a man named Joseph,
of the house of David.
The maiden's name was Mary.*

St Luke has no more to say about Zacharias and Elizabeth for the time being. His note establishes the background sufficiently for his readers to understand the coming reference to Elizabeth expecting a child in her old age. That done, he now settles into writing his record of the birth of Jesus.

He begins his narrative plainly, crisply, and with no frills. In two brief paragraphs, he sets the scene, establishing the time and the place. And names the two people so significantly involved in the event he is about to relate. He also sets the tone, the atmosphere in which the event he tells of occurred. For all the prosaic appearance of his introduction, St Luke is preparing his readers to see God taking a direct hand in the life and affairs of two very ordinary people.

The time is 'the sixth month'.

Because St Luke ends his earlier note with the statement that Elizabeth 'kept herself at home for five months,' it is tempting to reckon that he makes this time reference on the basis of Elizabeth's pregnancy. But that would be a mistake. St Luke is now embarked on a quite separate piece of history. And his 'sixth month' here has nothing to do with Elizabeth. It is calendar time.

The Jews had two calendars – the civil year and the sacred or ecclesiastical year. The sacred writers generally adopted the sacred calendar – e.g. Esther 3;7, 'first month Nisan'; 1 Kings 6:1, 'the month Zif, which is the second'; Esther 8:9, 'the third month, that is the month Sivan' etc. In the Jewish sacred calendar the sixth month is Elul. It was the twelfth month in the civil calendar of the times. Elul corresponds with our August/September. Elul, then, is the 'sixth month' to which St Luke is referring.

The place was 'a city of Galilee named Nazareth.' Nazareth was set on a rocky elevation, looking along a deep valley amongst barren, limestone hills. Nazareth's houses were built of the limestone quarried in the neighbouring hills. It gleamed white in the sunshine, and was known as 'the white city'. It was not, however, so remote as its being set in the hills might suggest. It was criss-crossed by the trade routes of the world.

Galilee, the province in which it was set, had the reputation of producing fearless men. Josephus says that they were 'warriors from infancy. Cowardice never had hold of them.' The town of Nazareth itself was legendary for its profligacy, as is reflected by Nathanael's later crisp quotation of the age-old taunt, 'can anything good come out of Nazareth?' The Talmud writes of the crimes of 'the white city on the hill'.

Now St Luke names the two people who played so prominent a role in the unique event in the history of mankind. 'A man named Joseph.' 'The maiden's name was Mary.'

But how little we know about them!

The New Testament reveals little or nothing about either of them. Most of the references are by St Matthew and St Luke, and the bulk of these is contained in the evangelists' record of the birth of Jesus. Outside of that, notices about Mary and Joseph are few and far between. The writers of the gospels were, clearly, not afflicted with a mania for biography. They tell what they consider necessary. No more.

What they tell us about Mary (*Mariam* in Greek; *Miriam* in Hebrew) is that she was a young woman living – presumably with her parents – in Nazareth. She had a sister, Salome, who married Zebedee of Capernaum, and was the mother of James and John. Mary was cousin to Elizabeth who lived with her priest-husband, Zacharias, in Juttah, and was the mother of John the Baptist.

In their presentation of Joseph, the evangelists are even more crisp and succinct. We learn that Joseph was a Bethlehemite, his father's name was Jacob or Heli, and he was a descendant of the House and lineage of David. That he stayed in Bethlehem a longish time following the decree of Augustus Caesar, suggests that he had relatives there, and lived at their house.

The writers of the Apocryphal Gospels, by contrast, however, are neither so reticent nor so inhibited as the evangelists. They are, indeed, lavish in the background they provide for Joseph. And they are no less generous – if not, in fact, imaginative and inventive – when they write about Mary.

Perhaps it's not out of place, here, to look briefly at what some of these authors were writing about Joseph and Mary – *The Book of James* (or *Protevangelium*) dated in the second century; *The History of Joseph the Carpenter*, in the fourth; *The Gospel of Thomas*, about the sixth century, and *The Gospel of Pseudo Matthew*, in the eighth or ninth century.

The History of Joseph the Carpenter, as its title implies, represents Joseph as a carpenter by trade and occupation. Which made him something of a rarity in Bethlehem, for Bethlehemites were famous for being stonemasons. Indeed, when Herod the Great was rebuilding the Temple, he used only the best materials, and the best craftsmen. He imported the timber into a country that was barren enough of suitable trees. And he recruited Bethlehemites as his stonemasons.

The Gospel of Thomas portrays Jesus as working in Joseph's carpenter's shop, and relates an episode which depicts Jesus looking for all the world like an eight-year-old wonder-boy.

Joseph, it appears, was commissioned by a rich man to make a bed. He set to work, but quickly realised that the beam he had prepared for the job was too short.

He was, not unnaturally, upset.

Until the eight-year-old Jesus came to the rescue, and advised Joseph to hold one end of the beam while he took the other. And, then, between them, they stretched the beam to the required length.

A grateful Joseph hugged him, and thanked God for giving him such a son.

The idea of Joseph as a working carpenter, and Jesus, in consequence, being a carpenter's son, once planted, stuck. Till, nowadays, we have latched onto it, and unquestioningly assume that that's how things were. And woe betide anybody who dares say differently.

But let us risk the woe betide, long enough to wonder if there might be another view.

Our Lord, during his teaching ministry, used all kinds of crafts and trades and occupations as illustrations – fishing, farming, shepherding, pig-keeping, stonemasonry and building houses, grinding corn, and repairing wine-bottles. But he never mentions carpentry or woodwork. Which seems strange if, in fact, Joseph had been a carpenter, and he himself had grown up learning the carpenter's craft.

Could it be, then, that in describing Jesus as 'the carpenter,' or 'the son of the carpenter,' we are doing the evangelists – and the translators – an injustice?

The difficulty stems from the bald, bold description in St Mark 6: 3 and St Matthew 13: 55: ' Is he not the carpenter?' and 'Is he not the carpenter's son?'

The face-value of the statements has to be treated with care. There's more here than meets the eye.

St Mark's account varies from St Matthew's, and may suggests either one or both of two possibilities. It could be that each evangelist was reporting separate observations by different members of the Synagogue congregation. It looks more likely, though, that it reflects the difficulty the evangelists had in conveying in Hellenistic Greek an expression which was typically Jewish and Aramaic. In much the same way as a translator, today, might have difficulty in expressing Shakespeare's 'A Daniel come to judgement,' in Chinese.

The Hebrew/Aramaic word *naggar* (carpenter) or *ben naggar* (carpenter's son) can have a metaphorical meaning in Jewish writings. *Naggar* can mean 'a learned man, a clever man, a man of wisdom'. Amongst the sayings in the Talmud is one which combines both expressions: 'There is no carpenter or carpenter's son to explain it.'

The expression is a compliment. There is also a derogatory expression – *Qoses ben qoses*, a cutter and the son of a cutter . It means someone despicable. It's meant to be derisory. And derives from the idea of the very worst thing a man could do to his neighbour – cut down his trees, the fig trees, the olive trees he depended on to make a living.

The comment reported by St Mark and St Matthew, as the context makes clear, is a reaction by the Synagogue congregation – in astonishment – to Jesus's 'wisdom,' and' knowledge,' and 'mighty works'. It is not a description of his craft, trade, or occupation. Nor of Joseph's, who, belonging to Bethlehem, the home of stonemasons, is more likely to have followed this craft.

Joseph is not mentioned in the list of names offered by either evangelist. And that's surprising, even allowing for the jaundiced view Nazarenes had of Jesus's birth, if all that's involved is describing a man's trade.

Exclamation marks in the English version might be better than question marks, and go some way towards easing the possibility of a misreading.

Take St Matthew's version of the episode as an example:

'He came to his native place, and taught them in their synagogue, so that they were amazed and said ...' The comments came from different people, in the atmosphere of the huddled-chatting that goes on after service. 'From where does he get his wisdom! And the mighty works! Is he not the carpenter's son!'

Astonishing! And even more astonishing because he's one of their own. They know his family. 'Is not his mother called Mary! And his brothers James, Joseph, Simon and Judas! And his sisters ... are they not with us ...! From where does he get all these things ...!'

St Matthew comments, 'They took offence at him.' The Greek word, here translated 'took offence', can suggest that Jesus was something of a 'stumbling block' to them. In Ireland, there's an expression which seems to fill the bill – 'They couldn't get over him.' And were not ready to accept him for the *naggar*, the *ben nagger*, the 'learned man,' the 'man of wisdom' that he was.

Our Lord's response hits the nail on the head. 'A prophet is not without honour except in his native place, and in his own house.'

Whatever craft, then, Jesus quite properly learnt as a Jewish boy, it doesn't seem to have been carpentry. Nor does carpentry appear to have been the craft by which Joseph earned his living.

Mary's parents, the Apocryphal Gospels inform us, are named as Joachim and Anna. If the tradition can be depended on, Anna was a serious and devout woman. Joachim was a rich farmer who lived well, and was generous with his wealth. He divided his income into three parts, giving one part to the Temple, one part to the poor, and lived on the rest himself.

The story is that Anna and Joachim, for years, were childless. And, because childlessness was viewed as a punishment from God for some hidden sin they had committed, they were ostracised and barred from the synagogue. Till, after twenty years of childlessness, their daughter Mary was born. After that, they had another daughter, named Salome.

When Mary was three years old, the writers tell us, her parents took her to the Temple to dedicate her to God and live and serve in the Temple. When they presented Mary, the priest sat her on the third step of the altar. She danced up fifteen steps, to the delight of the congregation,and never looked back. Joachim and Anna left, and went home praising God.

Mary, it appears, lived in the Temple till she was twelve years old, as one writer declares, or fourteen, according to another.

Whether at twelve or fourteen, the priests judged that she had now reached womanhood. And, in consequence, could no longer live in the Temple … for fear that she might pollute the holy place. The priests decided it was time to find a man – preferably a widower – who would marry her , and take care of her.

Enter Joseph.

Joseph was amongst the widowers summoned by the priests.

According to the *History of Joseph the Carpenter*, Joseph had married at forty. He had four sons – Judas, Justus, Simon and James – and two daughters, Lysia and Lydia. His wife died when they'd been married forty-nine years, while James was still young.

He had been a widower for a year when he was summoned by the priests.

He answers the call. And is chosen by lot to take Mary.

Joseph objects strenuously, on the grounds that he is an old man – by now he is ninety! – and Mary is but a girl. He would, he explains, become a laughing-stock to the Children of Israel. The priests, however, dismiss his objections, and force him to abide by their decision. Reluctantly, Joseph accepts, but with the *proviso* that some virgins should accompany Mary as chaperones. Rebecca, Sephora, Susanna, Abigea and Zahel are appointed.

Joseph takes Mary, along with her chaperones, to live in his house. But he as quickly leaves her there to go back to building his buildings. He was away two years. He returns, only to find the sixteen-year-old woman pregnant.

The authors write a great deal more, but the details need not detain us. Except, maybe, to round things off by noting that the *History of Joseph the Carpenter* reports that he lived to be one-hundred-and-eleven.

After all that imagination and invention, it's almost a relief to come back to the evangelist's starkly simple statement about 'a maiden betrothed to a man named Joseph … the maiden's name was Mary.'

St Luke, of course, is not burdened with what seems to be the apocryphal writers' urgency to establish that Jesus was not born of any physical union between Mary and Joseph.

The way St Luke presents the record argues that there is nothing out of the ordinary about the situation. Were it all so different, we would expect the painstaking St Luke to tell us so in so many words. And, certainly, if Joseph were, in fact, a ninety-year old widower with a ready-made family, it's unlikely that St Luke would have avoided mentioning it. The evangelist is careful in noting the old age of those who are old – as in the case of Elizabeth (1:18) and Anna (2:36).

What St Luke is describing is a quite normal arrangement between two ordinary people, a young man and a young woman, of not dissimilar ages – 'a maiden betrothed to a man named Joseph.'

St Luke's word to describe Mary as a 'maiden' or 'virgin' is the Greek word *parthenos*. The word can mean 'virgin' in the sense of a male or female without sexual experience, though it is not strictly limited to this meaning as the English word 'virgin' is. In the Greek translation of the Hebrew Bible (the *Septuagint*) *parthenos* is used to express any one of three Hebrew words – *'almah*, a young woman; and *na'arah*, a girl. For the most part, though, it is used for *betulah*. *Betulah* can mean a virgin in the sense of *virgo intacta*. It also describes a girl who has not attained puberty, and, therefore, is unable to conceive. The same word can also be applied to an unmarried woman who is expecting a child.

In deciding what St Luke means when he writes of Mary as a *parthenos*, it's important to notice the comment he attributes to her in verse 34: 'How will this be, since I do not know a man?' We may judge, then, that Mary was a virgin in the sense of being an unmarried, sexually inexperienced young woman.

The difficulty that some have, nowadays, in accepting the idea of the 'virgin' birth is really nothing new. They had difficulty in Mary's own day. Even thirty years after the birth, the people of Jesus' time dismissed the idea of a 'virgin' birth, and in their direct comments to Jesus himself made clear what they thought about his origins – 'we were not born of fornication' (Jn 8:41).

The evangelists do not have the same difficulty. They, however, are writing under the influence of their conviction that Jesus, after his crucifixion, was raised from the dead. A unique and supernatural exodus from the earth makes easily acceptable the idea of a unique and supernatural entry upon the earth. In the light of one, the other seems neither ridiculous nor impossible.

Betrothal or espousal was rather more than our modern

'engagement'. It was a binding contract to marry. And, while the contract did not permit cohabitation or allow the privileges of marriage, the woman was considered the man's lawful wife. She could not be put away without a bill of divorcement. And were she unfaithful to her betrothed husband, she would be treated as an adulteress.

Later on in the birth narrative, St Matthew writes of Mary as Joseph's 'wife'. He reports the angel's word to Joseph, making the point that Mary has not committed adultery: 'Joseph, son of David, do not be afraid to take home Mary your wife, for that which is conceived in her is through the Holy Spirit' (Mt 1:20).

The ceremony of betrothal was known as the 'making sacred', making the woman sacred to her bridegroom in every sense. It took place at the woman's father's house. The partners and their witnesses, in the presence of the synagogue elders and the leading men of the town, completed the contract under a canopy, set up for the occasion. Their friends and neighbours waited outside, to greet and cheer them after the ceremony … and join in the festivities which followed.

The ceremony itself was simple or elaborate, according to the taste, and perhaps the social standing, of the couple involved. Simply done, the man, in front of witnesses, presented the woman with a piece of gold or silver, and said, 'Receive this piece of silver (or gold) as a pledge that you shall be my spouse according to the Law of Moses.'

One tradition directed that the coin should be ninety grains of gold, another said half a grain of silver. Ultimately, however, the monetary value of the coinage didn't matter. The contract was bound by the giving and receiving of the token, be it gold or silver, or even no more than a *lepta* – a farthing – in value.

The betrothal coin, whether it was gold or silver or a poor man's *lepta*, gets honourable mention in our Lord's parable of the 'Lost coin' (Lk 15:8-9). For all the coins the woman possessed, the one she lost was her betrothal coin, her 'engagement ring'. And she reacted as any woman would in the circumstances. She turned the house upside down in her search. And when she found it, she called all her neighbours, 'Rejoice with me ... I've found the coin.'

The more elaborate arrangement involved drawing-up a written contract, signed by the man and woman themselves, and at least one witness:

'On ... day ... year, A son of B said to C daughter of D, be thou my spouse according to the Law of Moses and the Israelites; and I will give thee for the portion of thy virginity the sum of two hundred *zuzims*, as it is ordained by the Law; and the said C has consented to become his spouse on these conditions, which the said A has promised to perform on the day of the marriage. To this the said A obliges himself; and for this he has engaged all his goods even as far as the cloak he wears upon his shoulders. Moreover, he promises to perform all that is intended in contracts of marriage in favour of the Israelitish woman. Signed A, C, and witnesses.'

Some time elapsed – usually about ten months – between the day of the contract and the day of the nuptial celebrations. And that would be a great occasion.

The wedding ceremony could be held at the bride's home or at the groom's. Whatever home it was in, the groom and his family provided the feast. It was traditional for the wedding to be celebrated as the sun is setting. The guests, with their long-standing invitations, had been sent a reminder that the wedding was happening, 'Come, for everything is now ready.' Now they assemble, and await the bride's arrival.

In the bride's house, a proud, beaming, admiring mother supervises the young women as they put the finishing touches to dressing her daughter. They gabble and chatter as they work. Fixing, folding, smoothing, pleating, oohing and aahing at how lovely the brides looks. And then, with bright torches lighting the twilight sky, they rake the stillness, joining their singing with the flutes and pipes and drums, escorting the bride to the bridegroom's home, and her marriage.

When they see, coming towards them, the torchlights of the procession of his friends, bringing the bridegroom to meet her, the call goes up, 'Behold! the bridegroom comes. Blesssed is he who comes in the name of the Lord.' The two groups join and lead the bride and groom to the canopy where the wedding ceremony is performed. A simple ceremony in which the couple affirm their betrothal promises, and prayers are said, and blessings invoked, and the bride's father prays a benediction on his daughter.

Then the feasting begins. How long it lasts depends on the wealth and social standing of the families involved. It might last through the night. It could last for seven days for a virgin, but not more than three days for a widow.

When the party is ended, the groom walks with his newly-wedded wife through avenues of delighted neighbours to their matrimonial home. Cheering well-wishers strew their pathway with gifts of money and sweetmeats and flowers.

It was the day to look forward to and imagine during the months between the betrothal and the wedding. In the meantime, the bride-to-be gathered her 'bottom drawer.' Her betrothed was allowed to visit her in her father's house. But, in the eight days immediately preceding the nuptials, he was not allowed to visit.

This, then, is the situation with Joseph and Mary. They are betrothed, and now wait for the day of rejoicing, when they will be wedded, and Joseph will take Mary to their matrimonial home.

It is in this intervening time that the events occur of which St Luke writes.

How soon after the betrothal or how long before the wedding is difficult to settle. Nor are the evangelists concerned to pin-point the time. The events, so far as they are concerned, happened. St Luke is content to sum up in a few words everything that leads up to them: 'The angel Gabriel was sent from God to a city named Nazareth, to a maiden betrothed to a man named Joseph, of the house of David. The maiden's name was Mary.' However, statements in St Matthew's record – 'before they came together'; 'do not be afraid to take home Mary your wife'; 'When

Joseph woke from sleep he did as the angel of the Lord had commanded him, and took his wife home, but he did not know her
until she had given birth to a son ...' (1:18, 20, 24) – suggest that
the events occurred towards the end of the interval, if not, indeed, immediately prior to the already arranged marriage celebrations.

* * *

He went in and said to her,
'Hail, you who are favoured, the Lord is with you.'
She was perturbed at his saying,
and was considering what kind of greeting this might be.
The angel said to her,
'Do not be afraid, Mary, you have found favour with God.
You will conceive in your womb and bear a son,
and you shall call him Jesus.
He will be great, he will be called Son of the Most High,
and the Lord will give him
the throne of David, his father.
He will reign over the house of Jacob for ever;
there will be no end to his reign.'
But Mary said to the angel,
'How will this be, since I do not know a man?'
The angel answered her,
'The Holy Spirit will come upon you,
and the power of the Most High will overshadow you.
Therefore that too which is to be born
will be called holy, Son of God.
Also Elizabeth, your relative,
has conceived a son in her old age,
and this is the sixth month for her who was called barren;
for nothing will be impossible for God.'
Mary said,
'I am the Lord's servant;
let it be to me according to your word.'
Then the angel went away from her.

Did Mary know that the heavenly messenger was Gabriel who stood in the presence of God, and had been sent to bring momentous news?

St Luke does not explain. Nor does he hint that Gabriel revealed his identity in the course of the encounter. Indeed, quite the opposite. In St Luke's account, Gabriel seems to avoid the opportunity of identifying himself.

When Zacharias – from common sense, and his old man's understanding of the nature of things – has questioned the possibility of the message to him being fulfilled, he not only was told the messenger's name, but got a reprimand in the process, and paid the consequences of his doubting.

Mary, on the other hand, for all she asks a no less significant question, implying no less doubt, instead of a reprimand, she is given an assurance. But, without learning the messenger's name.

It's natural enough to wonder how, where and when the angel appeared to Mary.

Writing about Zacharias, St Luke notes the time, the place, and the fact that the priest, wide awake, performing his priestly duty, saw a figure standing on the right side of the altar of incense where no man ever stood.

We have no details, though, about Mary. No time, no place, no description of the physical surroundings. And no information about what Mary was doing or whether she was asleep or awake on this momentous occasion.

St Luke's presentation of the event gives the impression that Mary *hears* rather than *sees* the heavenly messenger. The feel of the piece, and the almost nightmarish tone of the experience strongly suggest that it all happened in a dream.

But it is, nonetheless, the message of God just because it was heard in a dream. Indeed, dreamtime is the appropriate time. The spiritual nature of the soul functions best when it is freed from bodily perceptions and physical distractions. And sleep is the likely time in which to find this freedom. And the message of God is heard in the dream of sleep.

Dreams as a way of communicating God's message are nothing new in either the Old or New Testament.

Amongst the instances mentioned in the Old Testament are the dreams of Jacob (Gen 27:10-15; 31:10-16), Joseph (Gen 11:5-11), Pharaoh's butler and baker (Gen 40:5-25), and Pharaoh (Gen 41).

In the New Testament, besides St Luke, St Matthew writes of dreams. They are all associated with the birth, the infancy and the sufferings of our Lord (1:20-24; 2:12, 13, 19, 22; 27:19).

Joseph's life is governed by dreams – to complete his marriage to Mary, the directions to him being communicated by an angel in a dream; to flee to Egypt to save the child; and, later, to return from Egypt. The Wise Men are warned in a dream to return to their homeland by a different route.

It is not out of place, then, to visualise Mary sleeping, and in the dream of sleep, hearing the angel speak the momentous message from God. For Mary, too, the course of her whole life is changed in a dream.

There is a blunt plainness in the way St Luke tells of it all, and, at first sight, it looks like an almost uninterrupted statement by the heavenly visitor. Which is natural enough. St Luke is preoccupied with the Divine activity rather than the human personality involved. At the same time, his approach is affected by the fact that he is presenting a report of the event, the recollection of the experience communicated directly or indirectly by Mary herself. And, in the telling, Mary has played down her own part in the encounter.

Maybe she did, but it is still difficult to imagine that so momentous an occasion, such an extraordinary announcement had no serious effect on the mind and emotions of the young maiden. She was too human to be expected to receive the angel's message with what, on a casual reading, appears to be equanimity. Emotionally, as the record suggests, Mary was alert, alive and sensitive. And the narrative itself, for all its clipped reportage, affords hints that the conversation in the lonely darkness of the night in Nazareth was not entirely lop-sided nor, indeed, so heavily weighted on the side of the angel as it looks.

To see it so, helps towards appreciating somewhat more keenly the tension and drama of the situation, and gaining an insight into the personality of the Virgin herself.

One thing more before we begin to try feeling our way around the picture St Luke paints of this unique event.

The whole episode is reported in direct speech, a presentation which gives the passage an almost naïve appearance: 'He said … The angel said … But Mary said … The angel answered … Mary said …'

St Luke, however, can do it no other way if he is to be true to his source. His arrangement stems from the fact that his presentation is either a translation or is based on a translation of a Hebrew/Aramaic document. And the Semitic idiom requires that all conversation be reported in direct speech.

The simplicity of the statement, however, ought not to be allowed to disguise the turmoil which so obviously tormented Mary from the beginning. There may be the odd spark of courage in it, but the whole episode is coloured by Mary's sense of fright, not to say consternation. Even the courage she shows is triggered by her fear. It is a long argument which ends with Mary capitulating.

'Hail,' St Luke reports, was the greeting which marked the angel's arrival. 'Hail, you who are favoured. The Lord is with you.' 'She was perturbed at his saying,' St Luke goes on, 'and was considering what kind of greeting this might be.'

'Hail,' 'Greetings' – St Luke's word *chaire* – translates the common Hebrew salutation *Shalom Lak*. St Luke's expression which we translate 'favoured' is a word which derives from *charis*, grace, and reflects the Hebrew word *chesed*, lovingkindness, the lovingkindness which marks God's relationship with his people, the favour he bestows upon them.

'Peace to you who are favoured of God. The Lord be with you.' That's the greeting. Gentle, kind, felicitous.

A greeting, though, is one thing, what lies behind it is another. Mary's awareness is sharpened, and she becomes conscious of the presence of the angel.

But, as her understanding of the scriptures taught her, angels are sent by God for a definite purpose. And those to whom they are sent must expect a message from God, a word either of reprimand or promise. There is every reason, therefore, for her mind to be racked, wondering what the visitation is all about. Does the heavenly messenger's arrival bode good or ill?

'Fear not, Mary ...' the angel encourages her. But the exhortation that she has no need to be frightened, for all its assurance that she has 'found favour with God,' is robbed of a deal of its comfort by the messenger's next bald, unbelievable statement. 'You are conceiving in your womb, and will bear a son.'

It's the kind of statement a young, unmarried woman wants to hear! And especially a young woman already betrothed, and with not much longer to wait till her wedding day!

It takes no great effort to imagine how Mary must have felt. It would need a piosity that has lost the habit of walking on the ground, and is far removed from the reality of human nature and emotions, to imagine Mary accepting the announcement serenely, with a wistful smile, and not a thought in her mind astray.

Like everything else about a dream, it takes no time at all to tell of all the action and talk when the sleeper is awake. But in the dream itself ... how long, how very long it lasts ... And the more strange, intriguing or frightening the dream, the longer it seems to endure.

The message which the angel spoke to Mary takes about a minute and a half to read aloud. And, no doubt, Mary, when she awakened, could relate it all quickly enough. But how long was the experience in the dream which Mary endured ...?

If the heavenly messenger makes what appears to be an uninterrupted speech, it can hardly have been because Mary was listening, rapt, spellbound in delighted wonder.

His announcement about her pregnancy is enough to flood her mind with a swirling stream of questions – the hurt it will cause Joseph, the man she dearly loves as he loves her ... the pain it will cause her parents, and the scorn they will suffer from mocking, gloating neighbours ... the damage and danger to herself, a young woman pregnant with a child while she waits to be married. And the stigma and consequences she must face for being judged as having been unfaithful to her betrothed husband.

The coming days and months and years would make her only too aware of the reality of things, and give shapes and sounds and faces to the frights and feelings of the dream.

For now, though, she must suffer the roar and rampage that possess her mind. And, speechless, tongue-tied, bear the weight of the fear and pain and fright that the angel's every uttered word pressed down upon her, layer by measured layer.

'You shall call his name Jesus. He will be great. He will be called Son of the Most High. The Lord will give him the throne of his father David. He will reign over the House of Jacob for ever. There will be no end to his reign ...'

Every fibre in her struggled to loosen her tongue and give her speech. Till, at last, she screeched out her plea, 'How can this be? I know no man.' Not any man ... not Joseph ... no man.

'The angel answered her,' and began to explain how it would happen that she would be with child. 'The Holy Spirit will come upon you, and the power of the Most High will overshadow you. Therefore that too which is to be born will be called holy, Son of God.'

Did she even understand what the angel was saying to her? It was certainly not the answer to the question she had asked, nor, indeed, the answer she expected to hear that would assuage her fears for Joseph, her family, and herself. The married were barren whom God did not bless with children, and would he give child to a maiden who was not married and had never known a man? The angel was telling her of things she could not understand, and spoke of things that, in her ordinary experience of life, were impossible, and beyond all the rules and ways of nature.

But the angel had been sent to tell her of things that seem to be impossible and outside the natural order. He cites the case of her cousin Elizabeth as an immediate and near-to-home illustration of what God the Almighty can do, and does, in what seem to mortals to be impossible circumstances. 'Consider your kinswoman Elizabeth. She has conceived a son in her old age. And this is the sixth month for her who was called barren.'

Offering Elizabeth as an example of God's almightiness is

hardly likely to help Mary feel the burden of her frights, fears, and anxieties have been lifted. In the gritty mundaneness of ordinary, everyday life, Joseph, her parents, and the neighbours are unlikely to be impressed with her assurance that God is doing great things for her! Old Elizabeth may well be, and beyond child-bearing age … But Elizabeth was married.

'Nothing is impossible for God,' is the word of the angel.

It is his last word. His final answer. There is no place, now, for debate or discussion. Whether she understands or not, whether she likes it or not, the course and pattern of Mary's life is sealed.

'Mary said, "I am the Lord's servant. Let it be to me according to your word".'

Centuries of piety have glossed this reply with an interpretation which implies that she happily and willingly accepted the situation.

The view is hard to understand. The tenor of the record, right from the beginning, suggests that Mary not only did not comprehend what was going on, but fiercely argued against what her reason told her was impossible, and her sense of propriety convinced her was improper.

Submissive she may have been, but only after a long struggle, and only after she had lost the battle. There is nothing she can do. There is no more she can say. And she yields to an authority too almighty for her to comprehend, in circumstances over which she has no control.

'I am the Lord's servant …'

The word we translate 'servant' is St Luke's word *doulé* (the feminine form of *doulos*, a slave). The word and its implications, in this instance, are significant. It carries the idea of a relationship of subservience, the subjection of the will. It suggests a relation of devotion, in which the devotee is at God's disposal, and is employed by him.

As St Luke reports it, the very expression which Mary uses is an act of total submission and subservience to the will of God. The words he represents her as saying paint the picture of her in the act of submission – head low bent and pleading, suppliant hands outstretched – 'Behold! The Lord's slave. Let it be to me according to your word.'

The tone of the submission would have echoes thirty years later. In Gethsemane. 'Father, if thou wilt, remove this cup from me. Nevertheless, not my will, but thine be done …'

St Luke completes this episode by reporting, 'The angel went away from her.' He begins the next with, 'During these days Mary rose up and made the journey with eagerness into the hill country, to a city of Judah. She went into the home of Zacharias and greeted Elizabeth.'

But how much is hidden in this narrow space.

St Matthew's record, though, complements St Luke's, and affords us details which fill out the events that occupy the 'in these days' of St Luke.

CHAPTER FOUR

Joseph's Dilemma
St Matthew 1:18-25

The birth of the Messiah was like this.
When his mother, Mary, was betrothed to Joseph,
before they came together,
she was found to be with child through the Holy Spirit.

Her husband, Joseph, being an upright man,
and unwilling to expose her,
wished to divorce her secretly.

He had these things in mind
but the angel of the Lord appeared to him in a dream,
and said,
"Joseph, son of David,
do not be afraid to take home Mary your wife,
for that which is conceived in her is through the Holy Spirit.
She shall bear a son,
and you shall name him Jesus,
for he will save his people from their sins."

All this took place to fulfil what was spoken by the Lord
through the prophet, who said,
'A maiden shall be with child and bear a son,
and they shall name him Emmanuel,
which is translated, God with us.'

When Joseph woke from sleep
he did as the angel of the Lord commanded him,
and took his wife home,
but he did not know her until she had given birth to a son;
and he named him Jesus.

St Matthew's record, clearly written from Joseph's side of events, offers a brisk summary of matters from the pregnancy to the birth in one fell swoop. And notes, at the same time, Joseph's naming of the child.

But the crisp telling hides a human drama of tears and fears and tensions.

A young woman, pregnant. Caught up in happenings she cannot understand, and which she cannot begin to explain without appearing to be wickedly arch or, worse, on the verge of lunacy.

And Joseph. St Matthew's account introduces Joseph as already knowing about the pregnancy. He also carefully writes, 'before they came together,' making it clear that Joseph and Mary were neither married, nor enjoyed the privileges of marriage.

How Joseph learnt about the pregnancy can only be guessed at. It may be that his *pronubae,* his 'go-betweens' who had arranged his marriage in the first place, advised him of the situation. It could well be that Mary herself told him in words she had rehearsed and doubly rehearsed, an explanation which, even to herself, sounded arch, naïve and ridiculous. It may be, of course, that Joseph noticed for himself. He wasn't blind. Human nature, however, being what it is, it's easy enough to assume that Jospeh learnt of Mary's predicament as the result of gossiping women of the neighbourhood. Women have a knack of knowing when another woman is pregnant. And seem to have uncanny knowledge if the woman in question happens not to be married.

However he heard, Joseph, not unnaturally, was unwilling to tolerate the situation. And they would hardly have been human had there not been some kind of confrontation. Mary trying to explain. Joseph finding everything impossible to comprehend and accept. He is a mere man, judging things as an ordinary man sees them. So far as Joseph was concerned, there was only one way by which a woman could be with child. And all the stories in the world about angels and angels' visitations could not convince him otherwise. On the face of it, Mary had been un-faithful to him. And, by the law, her unfaithfulness was as though she had been unfaithful to him as a wedded wife. She had committed adultery.

The problem, though, was easier to see than to solve. And the very fact that he had a choice of courses open to him merely complicated the situation for this 'upright man,' the innocent, law-abiding Joseph.

Regularising the marriage by cohabitation was not out of the question. It was acceptable practice in Israel. The Book of Tobit, in the Apocrypha, tells the story of Tobias and Sarah. They lived as man and wife, with no more formality than a blessing from Sarah's father, Raguel (Tobit 6-8).

It's hard, though, to imagine the idea crossing Joseph's mind as a solution. Apart from condoning another man's wrong-doing, Joseph could hardly be expected to marry Mary merely to legitimate another's offspring.

The law says he may divorce her. Precisely how he does this is up to him. He may sue her in open court. This would involve stating the cause. And, if Mary were to be proven guilty of adul-tery, she would be sentenced to death by stoning (Deut 22:23, 24). The partner of her crime would be liable to the same penalty. Mary, however, would have to endure the further degradation of having the sentence executed outside her father's house.

As an alternative to this, he could simply apply for a *Geth*, a bill of divorcement. He could choose to have the case heard in pri-vate. Under this arrangement, there would be no more witnesses than were essential to the case. A Rabbi would conduct the hear-ing, and there would be no need to state the cause of the suit.

The *Geth* simply stated the man's wish and willingness to be divorced from his wife:

'On such a day, month, year, and at such a place, I 'A' divorce you voluntarily, put you away, and restore you to your liberty, even you 'B' who was, heretofore, my wife, and I permit you to marry whom you please. '

The ceremony of delivering the Geth is simple, cold, and practical.

The Rabbi reads the document aloud. He instructs the woman to hold open her hands. He passes the document to the husband who then places it in his wife's open hands, with the words, 'Here is thy divorce. I put thee away from me, and leave thee at liberty to marry whom thou pleasest.' The divorcee wife closes her hands on the document in token that she receives it When the Rabbi has read the contents aloud once more, the divorce is complete.

And, whether the woman herself likes it or not, she is no longer married. She is allowed no defence. She has no opportunity to speak. She lives in a man's world, in a society where the grounds for divorce need be no stronger than that a man find something not pleasing in his wife (Deut 24:1).

Neither course, it would seem, appealed to Joseph. At the same time, though, he wants to abide by the law, and maintain his own integrity.

And here is Joseph's dilemma. This is the agony of mind he suffers as he thinks on these things, and searches for a solution.

It is not difficult for him to dismiss the idea of prosecuting Mary in open court. It's an open and shut case, as he sees it. The judgement clear and cruel. He could not even begin to contemplate being executioner of the woman he loves, and whom he once pledged – 'even as far as the cloak he wears upon his shoulders,' – to take as his wife. His love for Mary requires that justice be tempered with mercy and lovingkindness.

Yet the alternative piece of legality is hardly a solution either It is no more than a legal ploy. As Joseph knows to his sorrow. To become involved in that kind of legal exercise would be acting a lie, deceiving those who dispensed justice, and abusing the law he respected, and by which he lived.

Legal procedure, then, any kind of legal procedure is out. His conscience would not allow it. It would make Mary a scandal, and the butt of Nazareth's scorn.

But he still must find a remedy.

From somewhere in the thoughts that churned in his mind, the solution came to him. He would put Mary away 'secretly'.

He would let the contract to take her as his wife lapse, as though it had never existed. It would be quiet, without anybody, apart from their own small group, knowing anything about it. The matter would be entirely between Mary and her family, his *pronubae* , and himself.

In fact, though, it was no answer at all to his problem. It made only more difficulties. It would begin by robbing him of his integrity, and bringing him into disrepute for having re-neged on his marriage contract. It couldn't ease Mary's problem. It might divert attention from her. But only for a while. In the long run, it could mean for Mary only deeper degradation, more scathing ridicule, in a neighbourhood whose people would mis-read the good intentions of a generous, honest man as duplicity, and lace their hate with deadlier venom. It would also leave Mary, in her condition, bereft of the support of a husband, what-ever fault she had committed.

There was, in fact, no simple answer. Even marrying her would be no real solution. Amongst the begrudgers, backbiters and gossips in Nazareth, Mary's honour and respectability were already in tatters. Their marriage at this stage would only con-firm the conclusion about their relationship the neighbours had already drawn for themselves. And they would make sure she felt the barbs of their scorn.

Joseph's torment is ended in a dream. 'He had these things in mind,' St Matthew notes. They were churning in his mind. 'But the angel of the Lord appeared to him in a dream, and said, "Joseph, son of David, do not be afraid to take home Mary your wife, for that which is conceived in her is through the Holy Spirit".'

Nowadays, men don't readily accept the idea of finding an-swers to the crises of life in dreams. And, even less readily, approve the notion of having a conversation with God in their dreams.

To the Jews of Joseph's day, however, the proposition pre-sented no problems.

The distinction between today's thinking and the attitude in Joseph's time may stem from the fact that, with modern man,

God does not enter into their lives and thinking as God entered the lives of Jewish people in Joseph's day.

Joseph came of race of people who had lived with this principle. And he differed from them only slightly. A voice that his forefathers would, without hesitation, have ascribed to God himself, Joseph, out of reverence for a transcendent God, attributed to an angel, a messenger of God.

And the message brought by the angel, the instruction delivered to Joseph in his dream would, in no way, strike him as strange, or out of place in the scheme of things.

For Joseph, as for the rest of his race, the events of life, the ordinary happenings of ordinary people were under the control and direction of God. Everything in life had a divine significance. And if Joseph could not measure the precise significance of his immediate experiences, at the same time, he could hardly dismiss as of no importance what he presumed God was directing his attention to. 'She shall bear a son, and you shall call his name Jesus, for he will save his people ...'

It would be attractive to imagine that Joseph even vaguely saw the point and meaning of the angel's message. Like every single member of the Jewish race, he harboured the hope that Israel's Messiah would come. But, did it ever cross his mind that the woman to whom he was espoused, and was being directed, now, to marry, was to be the mother of Israel's Saviour, the very Messiah which he himself and his nation longed for?

Joseph's later history, however, suggests that, even when Jesus was growing up, he had no notion of what Jesus was about.

It is St Matthew, in an editorial note, who draws attention to the fact that what is happening is part of the divine will for Israel, and a fulfilment of Old Testament prophecy: 'A maiden shall be with child and bear a son, and they shall call him Emmanuel, which is translated, God with us.' He is recollecting the prophecy Isaiah had made some seven hundred years earlier, in the long-gone past of Israel's history.

Not every critic in the world today would agree with St Matthew's view of things. There are those who would strenuously deny that Isaiah's prophecy had any reference to Mary the Virgin and the son she was to bear. Rather, they argue, the prophesied birth was to be a sign to King Ahaz that God would fulfil his promise to deliver Judah from the invaders who threatened to overwhelm Jerusalem and the kingdom of Judah. The young woman might be any young woman of the time in Judah. Even the king's wife, or the wife of the Prophet Isaiah, or any young woman of the Royal House.

But, so far as St Matthew was concerned, in his day, the whole thing was clear-cut. As he understood it, Isaiah's prophecy was nothing less than the foretelling of the birth of Jesus Christ, the Messiah of Israel. The birth of Jesus to the Virgin was the fulfilment of God's long promise to Israel. His note is for the benefit of his Jewish-convert readers. He is at pains to help them to understand that Christianity is the true consummation of Judaism. Jesus is the Messiah of Jewish ancestry.

Joseph's reaction to the dream was the response of a righteous, law-abiding, God-fearing Israelite. He acted on the instructions. 'When Joseph woke from sleep, he did as the angel of the Lord had commanded him …'

If there had been any kind of confrontation when Joseph had first heard that Mary was expecting a child, it's natural enough to wonder how Mary reacted now, as Joseph told her of his change of mind.

Not all that long ago, this man could not believe her explanation because it involved a visitation by an angel from God. Now he wanted to marry her! Because his mind had been changed for him by an angel in a dream!

Irony, indeed. Which, when Mary recovered from the shock, and grasped what was happening, must have brought a smile to both their faces.

The wedding was on again!

How near was it all to the wedding day? Near enough, judging from St Matthew's report of the episode. His presentation suggests urgency, if not haste, in making the move.

The same nearness makes us aware of the torment Joseph

must have endured as he struggled in his dilemma to find an answer that would be kind to the woman he dearly loved. To say
nothing of Mary herself, and how she suffered her own hurt and
torment, innocent and blameless, on the other side of this unique
predicament.

'He got up,' St Matthew writes, 'and did as the angel of the
Lord had commanded him, and took his wife home ...' A quiet
enough occasion, it is fair to assume, in the circumstances. But
now they were married.

That told, St Matthew now seems to short-circuit things more
than slightly. 'He took his wife home,' he reports, 'but did not
know her until she had given birth to a son. And he named him
Jesus.'

St Matthew writes history in short spaces. He has us looking
at the end of the history before we've read of the happenings in
between.

No doubt, he was informed of all that happened in the 'in-be-
tween'. But, for reasons best known to himself, he doesn't write
about it. For those details, we have to depend on St Luke.

CHAPTER FIVE

Journey to Juttah
St Luke 1:39

*During these days Mary rose up
and made the journey with eagerness
into the hill country,
to a city of Judah.*

The marriage formalities are completed. There was no feasting. There was no appetite for it. No bridal walk through the town, along avenues bordered by happy friends and bubbling well-wishers. Shadows of suspicion smothered the gaiety that should have gilded and glittered the occasion. And sorrow fretted the minds of the innocent couple, characters in a drama which to them is still incomprehensible.

'He took unto him his wife.' They were married. It was sufficient. It was all they could ask for. And those who knew the cause of the suspicion felt relieved. Whoever had fathered the child, at least everything was wrapped in a cloak of respectability. And the young woman, when her time came, could be delivered of her child without too much guilt and shame.

The meantime, however, had yet to be lived through.

St Luke doesn't mention the marriage explicitly, as St Matthew does. His record, however, implies that it has taken place. And the readers of his day would readily have assumed this from his notice that Mary travelled the long journey alone. They would have known that as a 'maiden espoused', Mary would not have been allowed to make so long a journey unchaperoned. She could, though, as a married woman, undertake the trip unaccompanied.

Her journey to Elizabeth would take her about one hundred

and thirty miles from her home in Nazareth, along the trade route that ran from Damascus to Jerusalem. She would have to pass through Samaritan country, and up the fiercely steep road from Jericho to Jerusalem.

This was an infamous and notorious stretch of road. It was known as the 'Bloody Road', partly because, in the rains, its clay turned red, and the flooding water ran like blood. But that part was easy enough for travellers to bear. The more sinister reason for its name stemmed from the hazards and dangers travellers faced from the thieves and robbers and highwaymen who hid in the caves and crevices in the hills, and carried on their villany along the road, committing all kinds of atrocities. And who, if the need arose, had no compunction about murdering their victims. Not even priests and levites were safe on their way from Jericho to perform their duties in Jerusalem. And they were permitted – especially at the times of great Feasts, when the villains had a field-day – to carry weapons for self-protection.

It's the stretch of road that figures in our Lord's parable of 'The Good Samaritan.'

After Jerusalem, Mary would make her way further south to the hill country of Hebron. 'To a city of Judah,' is St Luke's note. 'Judah' or 'Juda' (*Iouda*) is likely to be a softened form of 'Jutta' or 'Juttah'. Juttah was situated south of Hebron. It was one of the cities of the priests who, like Zacharias, officiated in the Temple. (see Josh 15:55 and 21:6).

It was not an easy journey. Nor was it without its hazards and dangers and deprivations.

Maybe, then, it's not out of place to wonder why Mary decided to undertake it.

It may be that she did it on Joseph's advice, and with his encouragement. She would escape the gossip and tension in Nazareth. The marriage had solved no problems so far as the neighbours were concerned. It only robbed them of a scandal they might have relished and enjoyed. What was once just curious gossip that gave them the imagined right to pry and probe and ridicule, now truned to hate.

Being forced to endure the predicament may well have played a part in the decision-making. But it can hardly have been the main reason. Joseph himself, after all, was no less the butt of antagonism. Yet, he stayed in Nazareth.

It could be, of course, that she was doing no more than following the practice of a woman 'hiding' herself in the early days of her pregnancy (see Judges 13:13, 14). St Luke himself noted earlier that Elizabeth 'hid herself five months' after the realisation that she was to bear a son.

But, so long and hazardous a journey, as the trip to the 'hill country' would involve, seems an arduous undertaking for the sake of peace and quiet, and security against eating the wrong food. All that could have been managed away from Nazareth, without Mary being so far away from her husband and her home.

Did she go to her cousin Elizabeth, the wife of a priest, and a very much older woman, for advice and comfort in her condition?

How close Mary and Elizabeth were is an open question. The angel's reference to Elizabeth at the time of the annunciation may or may not mean that they knew each other all that well.

Whatever their relationship, though, it still seems a long journey when comfort and advice, like good food and safe drink, must have been already available close at hand. Traditon has it that Mary's mother, Anna, was a devout woman. And so devout a family must have numbered amongst its acquaintances nearby at least one godly matron who could have provided Mary with all the solace, advice and comfort that she needed.

Taking all in all, though, it would seem more likely that Mary's visit to Elizabeth was undertaken in order to assure herself of the truth of the angel's message.

It is the natural and obvious reason. And in keeping with what must have been Mary's reaction to the heavenly visitor that drew the recommendation in the first place. St Luke's statement that Mary went 'with eagerness' seems to support the view.

Mary wasted no time in going. To be assured that the message concerning Elizabeth was true and that she had understood it correctly, would go at least part of the way in helping her to understand and come to terms with her predicament.

Her later reaction in the *Magnificat* suggests that she found the assurance she had specially come to seek.

'Mary rose up and made the journey with eagerness into the hill country.'

In different and happier circumstances, she might have set out in a lighter spirit, and with even a sense of adventure. Her parents' farewell would not have been so sad. And parting from her newly-wedded husband – for how long she did not know – would not have wounded her heart so deeply and so cruelly.

She'd have rejoiced in the companionship of the women in whose group she travelled. Their husbands were amongst the men who travelled in a separate group, as custom and tradition dictated. It's unlikely that she was the only pregnant woman in the company. In different and happier circumstances, she'd have joined in the womany banter, swapping stories and comparing notes, and how long they had to go … and whether it was a boy or a girl they hoped for …

But Mary stayed on the edge of the banter. She couldn't join in. How could she? Her companions would ask questions. And how could she explain to them things she couldn't properly understand herself? She was married. That was sufficient for them. They accepted that. And assumed she was long enough married to be pregnant. And wasn't she the lucky woman to have a husband who loved her, and who followed the old customs, and let her get away for rest and quiet and to be cared for in the early days of her pregnancy. Even if it was so far away from home.

Things were best left like that.

The caravan settled into its own pace. Leisurely, but with a quiet sense of urgency. Nobody wanted to dally. Though the donkeys, laden with all kinds of paraphernalia, or carrying their riders, at times dictated policy. Where the going for them was rough, they went no faster than their good judgement guided them.

It was easy to spot the seasoned travellers. They were re-laxed. They knew the road, and how long the journey would take, and how far to travel each day. They knew the places to rest, and the *caravanserai*, the inns where the food was good, and the sleeping safe and comfortable in the cold nights. They rode easily, even when a recalcitrant mule, every now and then, halted the progress for a while.

There was music sometimes, when the men piped, their play-ing suited to the gait of the march. And the woman sang. Bright songs, sometimes, or crooning lullabies, making soothing com-fort for the infants in their arms.

It was a long road, a strange journey. Through villages and town and cities whose names were history, and shaped the story of her religion.

Dothan, where the fields were white with sheep, brought rec-ollections of the patriarch Joseph, and how his brothers had thrown him into a pit. And, then, rather than kill him, they sold him to a group of passing Midianite merchantmen who, later sold him to Potiphar, one of Pharaoh's captains in Egypt.

And the sad, sad region of Samaria. They were not welcome there. Not would they want to be. The Jews had no dealings with the Samaritans … as though they were entirely different races, entitled by nature to hate each other.

A quirk of history had shaped it so. How long, long ago! When Nebuhadnezzar had conquered the land, and carried off almost the entire nation into captivity and slavery in Babylon, some were left behind in Samaria. And those who were left be-hind intermarried with the conquerer. They mixed their blood with the blood of the heathen. They were no longer Jews. They were a heathen race.

All five hundred years ago. But, today, the travellers, though they might be starving, dare not eat food offered by the Samaritans. As if the Samaritans would even think about it! If Jews had no truck with Samaritans, then it was equally sure and certain that the Samaritans had no dealings with Jews. From the first day she could remember, Mary's religion had taught her,

'He who tastes the bread of a Samaritan, is as one who eats the flesh of swine.'

But they made a night-stop just beyond Sychar. It was the second halt of their journey. At Jacob's Springs, on the border of Samaria and Judah.

Jacob's well was there. The well, it was said, where the patriarch Jacob met and fell in love with his lovely Rachel.

It was, indeed, a love story.

Because Jacob could not pay the 'bride-price', he agreed to work for nothing for seven years to earn Rachel as his wife. But, on the night of the marriage, Laban, Rachel's father, tricked him. And gave him her older sister, Leah, instead. And forced Jacob to work another seven years for the privilege of marrying Rachel.

They talked about it over supper in the *khan* that night. And told it all again to their children before they went asleep. As though it had happened only yesterday.

And how Jacob, at Bethel, wrestled with the angel who would not tell him his name. But that night, Jacob's name was changed. Now he was called 'Israel'. He became the father of the nation of Israelites. From his twelve sons came the twelve tribes of the children of Israel.

And, to this day, all Israel recollected that night whenever they ate meat. They never would eat the sinew of the hollow of the thigh, because that's where the angel touched Jacob, and made him limp.

'A nation, a host of nations will come from you; kings will descend from you ...' was God's promise to Jacob, a voice in the group reminded them. And they all agreed that God had most assuredly fulfilled his promise to Jacob, as he had to Abraham.

Next morning, they left Samaria and the Samaritans behind. They were in Judah. And felt they were amongst their own again.

Now they were welcomed in the villages through which they passed. Children gathered them to greet them. Tousle-haired, barefooted, bodies gleaming brown with sweat in the sun.

Running alongside, almost the length of the village street, shouting, waving, being pushed aside now and again by the bigger ones, eager to sell their wares … trinkets, sweetmeats, grapes, fruit, vegetables …

Sometimes they stoppd in a village, and bought a cup of 'dibs' – grape syrup – that was refreshing, and left a lingering taste in the mouth. And they bought grapes and cucumbers to eat along the way.

The road was a busy place. A highway of caravans of people coming and going. Merchants, businessmen, ordinary folks, pilgrims making their way to and from Jerusalem. And a mass of colours. Reds and greens and blues and yellows on the women. The grand merchants in their white robes and yellow headscarves, the burning scarlet saddles on their grey horses. Homely, dull-brown camels graced their way, dwarfing the camel-drivers' donkeys, riding in front of them, leading the train. Herds of black goats, and bulky red oxen lumbering along. Shepherds in their short cloaks, yellow or red kerchiefs over their heads, falling down the neck and shoulders. And sheep, slowly nibbling as they went, their shepherds watching, keeping them within whistling distance. It was like a moving market-day.

A troop of Roman cavalry passed them, escorting a line of mule-drawn supply wagons, heading towards the north. Friendly men they were, for all they rode their mounts with pomp, pride, and soldierly alertness. Their lances and spears, their shields and helmets silver-glancing in the sun. They were obviously on serious business. And the guess amongst the travellers was that they were on their was to Sepphoris, not far from Nazareth. It was the obvious place. The Roman army had an arsenal there. The children waved to them, the lads standing smartly, and saluting. And the officer leading the troop, saluted, no less smartly, back, a broad grin wrinkling his clean-shaven face.

It was bare, barren hills, and hot ground, burnt dusty by the sun, that faced Mary and her companions as they journeyed on.

And, though, they might feel eager to get on to Jersualem, they were glad to rest awhile in Shiloh. The seasoned ones amongst them knew where the shade was, and encouraged everybody to eat, and then try to get an hour's sleep. That would refresh them.

In Shiloh, like everywhere else along their route, the travellers scuffed their sandals with the centuries-worn stones of their people's history.

It was in Shiloh that Hannah, after years of childlessness, pleaded with God for a son. And she gave birth to Samuel who became a prophet of Israel. He anointed Saul, the son of Kish, as Israel's first king.

It's impossible to think that the travellers didn't talk about it all. And recollect the stories and history they had grown up with in their synagogues. Stories of the days long before Solomon built the Temple in Jerusalem, and there was a temple in Shiloh, where the Ark of the Covenant was safely and devoutly housed.

Did Mary, in her own situation, think of Hannah? And wonder at the irony of things. How a years-long married woman had to plead with God to bless her with a child, and she herself had conceived without ever having known a man ... at God's own direction and dictation ... 'How unsearchable are God's judgements, and his ways past finding out.'

And did she, while she rested in Shiloh, recollect the words of Hannah's prayer of thanksgiving ... long enough and deeply enough for them to find echoes later on in her own prayer in Elizabeth's house?

It was on, now, to Jericho, and the long climb which, the seasoned ones advised them would be hard and tiring. But they softened the harshness with the comfort that, at the end of it all was Jerusalem.

Jericho itself ... or rather ... the new Jericho, not long founded and completed by Herod, king of Judaea, was a beautiful city.

'A scented garden in the wilderness,' is how it was described. 'God's Garden.' And it was. The heady scent of balsam groves filled the sky, and the aromas from the blossoming gardens teemed in the warm air.

It was built alongside the ancient ruins of the former city which Joshua besieged for seven days, and then destroyed. The old city was small, covering about six acres. It was surrounded by two perimeter walls. The inner wall was twelve feet thick, the outer six. As defence walls, they were thick enough, and may well have appeared solid enough. But they were poorly built, on a foundation of debris.

The deliberate and purposeful tramping of thousands of feet every day for seven days, cannot but have affected the standing of the walls. And the great, bellowing roar of two thousand voices on the last day, sent the walls hurtling, like an avalanche, to destruction.

Herod might have built his new Jericho on the ruins of the former city. But not even Herod would presume to risk the curse Joshua had pronounced on anyone who attempted to rebuild it.

Instead, he built alongside the old city. And what he built was magnificent. Laid out squares and avenues. Groves and gardens. Majestic buildings. Built to last for ever, from limestone quarried in the surrounding hills. An amphitheatre where Herod, when he stayed in the city, arranged circuses for the people. And which the poeple attended in their droves, flouting their Jewish law, ignoring the anathemas of their hierarchy. And a hippodrome that roared with the noise and fear and excitment of chariot races.

But all at what a cost …? A crippling tax to pay for it all. Which was an added reason for his subjects to hate the king. But add to all that, the cost in human pain and degradation and suffering, and death. The men who slaved in Herod's huge labour force, and died quarrying limestone from the hills. The scorched, scabbed bodies of broken men who toiled in the killing sun, scraping in the rock-hard ground, to shape the aquaducts that brought water to the king's groves from Elisha's Pool.

It was comman gossip that, if the king were not obliged and expected to live in Jerusalem, Herod would have reigned from Jericho. Of all the cities he had built, Jericho was his favourite.

And Mary and her companions were inclined to agree with

him. And might have dallied to enjoy the city were their minds not set on getting to Jerusalem before the sun had set.

As it was, they dallied long enough. Gawping and gazing. And where they didn't dally, they were delayed by thronging people as they tried to make their way through crowded streets to the city gate. 'God's Garden' it might well be, but it was crowded. Where the broad squares, lined with trees, and the wide streets ended, the tight-packed alleyways of the marketplace began.

Bustle took over from the comparative peace. The smells and stagnation of the market suffocated the scents and aromas. And the drone of noise was everywhere. The raucous bellowing of merchants, the barking din of scavenger dogs, the frantic, frightened sound of animals being herded through the unyielding chaos of people.

They made no delay, now, getting through the gate of the city.

Outside the gate, they were glad to sit and rest. Not that they were the only ones. There were groups and bands all over the place. Some quiet and serious. Others laughed loudly and were so obviously enjoying everything. Some, though, were raucous and noisy, signalling to all around that they'd had more to drink than was good for them. And embarrassing their quiet neighbours around them.

One of the seasoned ones of the company had found a clump of fig trees, and shooed out of the boughs the few goats who were working their way steadily through the burgeoning crop. It was cool in the little shade the trees gave from the hot sun. So they were no sooner sitting than they began to eat. Bread, still almost hot from the bakery, dipped in the syrup, made good eating. And they relished it. Then cooling melon and cucumber.

All the time, they received full, if still wary, attention from scavenger dogs and goats on the prowl for throw-away scraps.

Bright-eyed, street-wise, insistent urchins paid frequent visits, urgent to sell trashy trinkets. And fruit which looked as though it had waited a long time to be sold. But they were careful to hold it so that the best part showed.

Some of the company slept after they had eaten. But now, it was time to be on the move again. And they were ready to face the climb to Jerusalem.

Churning the dust on the road ahead of them was a band of people. And by the time they were well on the way, another company of travellers was following behind.

They greeted those who passed, coming down the hill. And a small group of priests and levites on the way back to their homes in Jericho, having completed their spell of duty in the Temple.

The men in Mary's company piped as they rode. Slow tunes they were, for it was a slow, sapping, wearying march they played for. The women didn't talk much, though the nursing mothers crooned or murmured to their infants, keening with discomfort, and waved gentle hands, wafting away the forever marauding flies.

The climb seemed to go on for ever. The pilgrim song about being 'glad when they said unto me, "let us go up to the House of the Lord",' lost some of its charm in the heat and sweat and tiredness, and the itching, invisible flies. And the soreness of riding between panniers on a donkey's back.

The piping men no longer piped, worn and tired. And everyone was glad when an obstinate mule stopped, and brought the whole company to a halt. The nursing mothers took the chance to settle their discomfited infants. The seasoned travellers, more used to these things, did a quick dismount to stretch their legs and shake their arms to relieve the strain of riding. But the stops, they reckoned, were never long enough.

To their right, the stretching wilderness climbed the hill alongside them. And, on their left, far, far below, the Salt Sea, where the Jordan river ended its twisting and turning, fertile and verdant way all the country long, from Chinnereth, the harp-shaped Sea of Galilee.

The cheers and shouts from the group ahead signalled that they'd reached level ground at last. The news didn't make the climbing any easier for Mary's company. But it brought a lightness. Even the animals seemed to react brightly.

The piping began again, giving new spirit and purpose to the march. And they found energy enough to cheer and shout and rejoice when they themselves came to the level ground.

They needed no encouragement to quicken their pace when they saw the *khan*, the inn, at the side of the road a little way ahead.

While the men worked – loosening the saddle straps, watering and feeding the animals – the women washed, bathing their hands, splashing refreshing coolness on their faces, bathing the dust and heat from their feet. And then, they sat down in the cool shadow of the wall, and ate and drank with relish, the food and wine the serving-girls brought them.

The guffaws and banter coming from the men's group near-by, meant they, too, were being plied with food and drink.

It would have been easy to stay and enjoy the comfort of the place. But, it wasn't yet journey's end. There was still Bethany. And then it would be Jerusalem, with a night's rest, and sleep in a real bed. And those who knew about these things, said that, from here on, it was downhill all the way.

There wasn't much more travelling to do, and everybody was anxious to get to Jerusalem while it was still day. The men and the inn-lads checked the straps and saddles and panniers on the animals, and the company was on its way again.

Bethany was beautiful. A little village, green and serene. A delight of date-palms, fig trees, olives, and flowers in profusion blooming. So much life and loveliness on the edge of burnt, barren wilderness.

They took the longer way down to Jerusalem from here. There was another route that was much shorter, but it was steep, steep … and they'd had enough of steep hills for a while. The way they took would mean more time, but it was a soft-sloping road that wound gently down the mountain side. And it was worth it. As they turned in the bend, there, spread out below them, was Jerusalem. Shapes and shadows in the sun, and the roof of the Temple gleaming.

They crossed the bridge over the river Kedron – no more,

really, than a half-dried wadi – and they were through the gate and into the city.

But it was more than that. They had come through the gate in the great wall that formed the boundary of the east side of the Temple precincts. Now, they were in Jerusalem. And they rejoiced. They stood on Mount Zion. And they were glad. The toil and hardship of the climb had been worth it. 'Our feet shall stand within thy gates, O Jerusalem.'

A different time, and in different circumstances, Mary could have been moved and exhilarated by it all. But not now. There was too much on her mind to let her even think of rejoicing. And she was urgent to get to her cousin Elizabeth.

The bulk of the company had reached their destination when they'd arrived in Jerusalem. Some lived in the city. Some were pilgrims. A few would be travelling further on, after they'd stayed a few days in the city.

A couple of the women guided Mary through the city. And she was grateful. A stranger in the place, she'd never have found her way through the labyrinth of streets. They brought her to the gate at the south west corner, and set her on the road to the hill country, and Juttah. A few more miles to go. But she was on her own, now.

Not far out from Jerusalem, on the road towards Bethlehem, she came to the Pillar of Rachel's Grave. She stopped long enough to respect the memory of a woman whose name, and the names of whose sons were still mentioned with reverence, honour, and thankfulness throughout all Israel.

The history of her nation told her why Rachel was buried here, at the side of the road. Jacob, her husband, an old man by now, was moving his family from Bethel. Rachel his wife was expecting a child, and,along the journey to Ephratha – Bethlehem – she went into labour. She gave birth to her second son. But now she was dying. And, in her dying breath, she named her son Ben-oni, the son of my sorrow. Jacob, though, changed the name to Ben-jamin, the son of my right hand, or even the son of good luck.

Did Mary, as she travelled the road alone, wonder how God, according to her nation's history, seemed to choose once-barren women to be the mothers of the great men of Israel? Women like Sarah, who had laughed at the promise of bearing a son at her age. Or Hannah whom Shiloh must have brought to mind. Or, now, Rachel, as the tomb she stood beside reminded her.

Did she wonder if the child promised to the long-barren Elizabeth and the aged Zacharias would be great amongst the people of Israel?

Did it even fidget at the edge of her mind what was his purpose in giving child to a young woman who was a virgin, and had never known a man?

The little town of Bethlehem was next, nestling amongst the hills. What sad sense of loneliness overtook her as she passed through the hometown of her husband, Joseph.

Then on to Hebron, and through the quiet village to Juttah.

The long journey in the scorching sun was over. The rough camps in the bleak, cold nights were gone. Tonight she'd be amongst friends.

Suddenly, she was tired. It was the tiredness she had struggled with all the journey long. She shook herself, and rubbed her eyes. The dust of travel was in her face.

She pulled her cloak, comforting, about her, and urged the donkey faster. She would be in her cousin Elizabeth's house before the darkness.

CHAPTER SIX

With Elizabeth
St Luke 1:40-56

She went into the home of Zacharias
and greeted Elizabeth.
When Elizabeth heard Mary's greeting, the child leapt in her womb
and Elizabeth was filled with the Holy Spirit.
She cried out with a loud voice,
'Blessed are you among women,
and blessed is the fruit of your womb.
Why has it happened to me
that the mother of my Lord has come to me ?
For as the sound of your greeting came to my ears
the child in my womb leapt for joy.
Blessed is she who believed,
for there will be a fulfilment
of what has been spoken to her from the Lord.'

How soon Mary found Zacharias's house, or who told her
where in the village it was, St Luke leaves to his readers' wit and
imagination. 'She went into the home of Zacharias,' is all he
writes.

It's natural to assume that Zacharias met her as she entered,
and made her welcome, communicating as best he could, since
he was dumb, and could not speak. Mary must have been surprised, not to say intrigued, that Zacharias, still actively involved in the priestly ministry of the Temple, could not speak.

It's likely that he wrote on a tablet to explain things. He was
to use one, later on, to communicate his wishes at the naming of
his son. And the tablet, on that occasion, seems to have been
quickly and readily available. It's safe, then, to reckon that he'd

formed the habit of using a tablet to communicate during the six months since he was deprived of his speech. And it's not pressing things too far, then, to suggest that this was how he greeted Mary, and explained the situation.

She is shown all the customary courtesies afforded a welcome guest, especially a guest at the end of a long journey.

But St Luke takes all this as read. He is urgent to get on reporting the meeting between the two women.

Taken at face value, St Luke appears to be doing no more than reporting Elizabeth's excitement at Mary's unexpected arrival. So excited is she, that the baby in her womb kicks furiously. And, then, as though she were in another room, she shouts loudly enough for Mary to hear. She tells Mary of her delight at the visit, and how the baby had leapt in her womb when she'd heard the greeting. And, in a few apt and pious words, she encourages Mary to hold on in sure hope and confidence that all will be well. God is faithful.

Mary responds. No less piously, though her words, for what looks like an off-the-cuff response, still have a poetic look and feel about them.

The conversation between the two women – allowing for the odd emphatic pause, and a silence here or there – lasted two or three minutes.

And that, on the face of it, is all that happened in the whole of the three months Mary stayed with her cousin Elizabeth.

But, leave things like that, and we miss the point St Luke wants to make in this so brief episode.

St Luke is, so obviously, not interested in writing up all the details of the visit, the ins and outs of what went on during Mary's three-month stay. What he is concerned about is establishing that Elizabeth, in a prophetic ecstasy, is nothing less than the mouthpiece by which God confirms his word and will to Mary.

By way of an introduction, St Luke explains that 'When Elizabeth heard Mary's greeting, the child leapt in her womb.'

This, as far as it goes, need express no more than the natural reaction to sudden excitement by any woman well on in her pregnancy.

The evangelist's completion of the paragraph, however, suggests that he invests the occurrence with a somewhat different and deeper significance. He writes, 'Elizabeth was filled with the Holy Spirit, and spoke out with a great voice.'

The statement can mean only one thing: Elizabeth, for this brief moment at any rate, is a prophetess, 'filled with the Holy Spirit'. She is in the great tradition of the Old Testament prophets. The 'great voice' with which she speaks out is not just a loud voice in order to make herself heard. It is the 'great voice,' the *Bath Qol, the daughter of a voice, the echo of the voice of God,* the sound by which God, through his prophets, is understood to communicate to men. (see Ps 68; Ezk 1:25; 10:5; 43:2; Dan 11:31; 2 Pet 1:17; Rev 16:17; 21:3).

St Luke underlines the point by noticing Elizabeth's interjection in the middle of her prophesying. She explains to Mary, 'As the sound of your greeting came to my ears, the child leapt in my womb for joy.'

It looks like a repetition of what St Luke has already written about Elizabeth's reaction earlier on. And it is. But with a significant addition.

As Elizabeth tells it, the baby didn't just leap in her womb. It leapt *'for joy'*. And there's the difference. *'For joy,'* translates St Luke's expression, *'in wild joy,'* – from *agalliasis, wild joy, ecstatic delight.*

Now it reads, 'The child leapt in my womb *in an ecstasy.'* And the impression that St Luke leaves is that Elizabeth, in the very act of prophesying, suddenly becomes aware of the import of what she is saying. She interrupts herself. 'Why has it happened to me that the mother of my Lord has come to me?' And, in the same moment, she recognises her experience on Mary's arrival as an overwhelming religious experience. An ecstasy. And in this ecstasy, Elizabeth echoes the word from God to Mary.

If Mary had come to Juttah for confirmation of the message transmitted to her by Gabriel a short while earlier in Nazareth, she was now having confirmation in earnest. 'Pressed down, shaken together, and running over.' Elizabeth's condition was clearly obvious. And God's hand in the matter had been explained by Zacharias. But, added to this, there now came the word of confirmation, unexpectedly from God.

Elizabeth's prophecy itself is a reiteration – if not in every instance verbatim, at least in sense – of the salient statements in the earlier message of the angelic visitor:

Blessed are you among women.	You who are favoured.
(v. 42a)	(v. 28)
Blessed is the fruit of your womb.	… that too which is to be born
(v. 42b)	will be called holy …
	(v. 35)
There will be a fulfilment	Nothing will be
of what has been spoken	impossible for God.
to her from the Lord.	(v.37)
(v.45b)	

Mary is afforded assurance about her child, 'blessed of God (*eulogemenos* from *eulogeo*, to bless) is the fruit of your womb.' A consolation that would rejoice her mother's heart. She is given a double assurance about herself which, in the circumstances, is no strange thing. 'Blessed of God (*eulogemene*) are you among women' – an assurance her mind would need, and be glad of, since she could not fully comprehend, let alone explain, the fathering of her child.'

Then follows the assurance that what has been promised by God, he can and will most assuredly accomplish. The word of encouragement to Mary is that when God's purpose has been finally fulfilled, 'Blessed she that believed.' Here, the English word 'blessed' is a rendering of a quite different word in St Luke's record of the threefold blessing.The word he uses now is *makaria*. It means *happy, to be envied*. Women would envy her for the honour conferred on her, and the part she was chosen and allowed to perform.

Mary had found what she needed. For, if what the vision in Nazareth had revealed about Elizabeth were true, she could begin to dare to have confidence that the rest would be true also.

Her whole situation had changed. The dread was gone. She was no longer in fear about the child she carried. No longer a degraded woman. Elizabeth's prophecy had echoed the promise God had made through his angel. She was, indeed, a woman to whom God had shown favour.

> *And Mary said,*
> *My soul declares the greatness of the Lord,*
> *and my spirit rejoices in God, my Saviour,*
> *because he has looked favourably*
> *on the lowly condition of his servant.*
> *From now all generations will call me blessed,*
> *for the Mighty One has done great things for me.*
> *His name is holy,*
> *and his mercy is for generation after generation*
> *towards those who fear him.*
> *He has acted powerfully with his arm:*
> *He has scattered those who are proud*
> *in the thoughts of their mind;*
> *He has brought down rulers from their thrones,*
> *and the lowly he has raised high;*
> *He has filled the hungry with good things,*
> *and he has sent the rich away empty;*
> *He has come to the aid of his servant Israel,*
> *in remembrance of his mercy*
> *(as he spoke to our fathers)*
> *towards Abraham and towards his descendants for ever.*
>
> *Mary stayed with her about three months*
> *and returned home.*

The message through Elizabeth eased the tension, and Mary could relax. There was a sense of sweet relief. In these circumstances, it's natural to see what St Luke writes now – the *Magnificat*, the 'Virgin's Song' – as Mary's immediate reaction to Elizabeth's prophecy, her song of sheer joy and relief, a fountain of words bursting the safety-valve that had held her emotions too long under too fierce pressure. Yet, was it?

But, before trying to answer that, it's important to have in mind that there are those who suggest that the *Magnificat* was never part of the original gospel according to St Luke. It crept into the text later, they suggest. Others argue that it was spoken, not by Mary, but by Elizabeth. There is some manuscript evidence supporting 'Elizabeth', but the evidence is weak.

That said, then, the general view is that it's fair to judge that the words were, in fact, spoken by Mary herself.

But when? St Luke's blunt 'And Mary said ...' suggests that the words need not have been an immediate reaction to Elizabeth's prophecy.

Compared with the other speeches which St Luke reports in his record, Mary's song is too long and ponderous to be a spontaneous response to Elizabeth. And that Mary should not respond immediately, whatever her emotions, seems to be in keeping with the pensive and thoughtful nature of the Virgin as St Luke portrays her. For example, surprised as she was by the visit of the angel, her response is slow. And even then, she speaks only when she has struggled with things in her mind. And again, after the incident with the boy Jesus in Jerusalem, St Luke writes of Mary that she 'kept all these sayings, and pondered them in her heart.'

If it is not an immediate and spontaneous reaction, is it possible, as some suggest, that it was not a single, complete speech? Could it be an accumulation of thoughts and feelings which Mary expressed at various times during her stay in Juttah, and which have been arranged by St Luke into a composite piece?

Maybe it was. At the same time, though, there's nothing in the world to say it wasn't a piece which Mary carefully and deliberately composed during her stay with her cousin. She stayed with Elizabeth and Zacharias three months.

Take stock of the atmosphere in which she was living. See the two people who afforded her such caring friendship, and gentle, generous hospitality. Zacharias, the priest, who himself, hour by hour and day by day, intimately experienced God's hand and direction in his life. And Elizabeth, his wife. Herself a daily example of the strange ways of God. Both of them living proof of God's intervention in the lives of ordinary people.

There was peace in the house, and strengthening comfort in the company of the older woman. Expecting a child herself, made Mary's cousin understanding and sympathetic.

In the tranquility, there was time and opportunity for Mary to think and talk and meditate.

If she had time to measure her experiences, her feelings, and God's intervention in her life, then, there was, surely, time enough for her to shape her meditations into the order in which St Luke presents them here.

In deciding when Mary spoke the words, it might be helpful to take our cue from the statement St Luke uses to close the episode: 'Mary stayed with her three months, and returned home,' he writes. And coming, as it does, immediately after Mary's words, gives the impression that Mary spoke them to her cousin just before she left to go back home to Nazareth. Mary's speech was a parting word to Elizabeth.

The *Magnificat*, however, could hardly be described as an original composition. It consists mainly of thoughts sparked and shaped by the Psalms and the Prophets. There is artistry, though, in the way the thoughts are chosen, and eventually blended together to form a prayer of thanksgiving that rests, gentle, in the mind, and yet trips, fervent, from the lips.

It comes out of long, slow, contemplative meditation which Mary had time and space for in Juttah. The announcement of the angelic visitor still hangs in her mind, and the word delivered to Joseph in his dream. All mingling with Elizabeth's threefold blessing – blessed are you among women; blessed is the child you carry; blessed will your future be when God fulfills his purpose.

For all she sees in Elizabeth that the angel's words are true, for all she hears the blessing Elizabeth announces, she must still attempt to accommodate her heart and soul to something which is way beyond her comprehension. She is making the pilgrimage of a suppliant, seeking strength and assurance ... even without fully understanding.

In her contemplation, her pilgrimage, she finds solace and consolation in the scriptures and prayers of her well-practised religion. And a means of expression in its familiar language. Her religion and her religious upbringing have taught her about God's intervention in the lives and world of ordinary people.

And if she needed a reminder, the journey that had brought her to Juttah from Nazareth did just that.

She had tramped the long road marked with the memorials of her nation's history, and the signals of God's hand – the 'mighty hand and oustretched arm' – directing and protecting the life and affairs of her people, the whole nation of the people of Israel … Abraham and her forefathers, all Abraham's descendants. Including herself.

Shiloh, along the journey, cannot have failed to bring Samuel's mother, Hannah, to her mind. And, almost instinctively, she would have recollected Hannah's prayer of praise and thanksgiving which, as a young devout Jewess, Mary heard constantly and regularly at synagogue services.

Hannah's prayer served as her model, if not, indeed, as her inspiration to shape the expression of her own thoughts.

Look at the prayers of both women, and Hannah's influence in clearly obvious in the thanksgiving which Mary composed. Not only is the shape there but echoes of Hannah's words and ideas are clear to hear.

Almost every line in Mary's *Magnificat* can find a reflecting reference in 1 Samuel 2; Psalms 33 and 34; and Isaiah 52 and 54.

But that's not surprising.

The reference in 1 Samuel is, of course, the record of Hannah's own *Magnificat*. If Hannah's prayer of thanksgiving was Mary's model and inspiration, it's only to be expected that Hannah's words and sentiments are part of Mary's composition. Indeed, the opening statements in both prayers are almost identical. In Hannah's prayer it's her 'heart' that exults; in Mary's it's her 'soul.'

The passages from Isaiah and the Psalms are passages of the scriptures made familiar by their frequent repetition at Synagogue services. Psalms 33 and 34 formed part of the daily and early morning services, and especially the Sabbath service. Isaiah 52, besides being a reading in Synagogue, was also a passage to be read or recalled on any occasion when comfort is needed. Isaiah 54 was a scripture passage read frequently throughout the year as a second lesson at Sabbath service.

In Mary's circumstances, it seems fair to judge, recollecting such familiar scriptures would be natural, appropriate, and almost instinctive.

And the passages, once called to mind, would be mulled-over again and again.

Hear Mary's thanksgiving, and it's like hearing clear echoes of Isaiah fifty-four. Isaiah's prophecy is the pulse that beats all through the song. Even the train of Mary's thought follows the sequence of the Prophet's message.

It's as though, in her pilgrimage, Mary feels Isaiah's words as applicable and appropriate to herself in her situation and predicament: 'a woman forsaken ... and grieved in spirit ... for a small moment have I forsaken thee ... I hid my face from thee ... afflicted, tossed with tempest and not comforted ...' (Is 54:6, 7, 8, 11).

At the same time, it holds for her – whenever she learns to recognise it, under Elizabeth's godly counselling – the vital word of promise, the strengtening, supporting assurance.

And she has Elizabeth to lean on. Wise, comforting Elizabeth, gently, slowly taking her young cousin, like a disciple, through the angel's message. All the time shaping, wondering, suggesting, here feeling after, there probing, till the words begin to have a new dimension. And persevering with Isaiah's prophecy. Seeking, beyond the sound of dereliction, to hear the ringing tones of promise, hope and reassurance in the Prophet's message. 'Thy maker is thy Lord ... the mountains may depart, and the hills be removed, but my kindness shall not depart from thee, neither will my covenant of peace be removed ... every tongue that shall rise against thee thou shalt condemn ... this is the heritage of the servants of the Lord ...'(Is 54:5, 10, 17).

And while she couldn't always readily share the dazzling

vision as Elizabeth interpreted the Prophet, yet it was no longer so frightening to her. And as the days grew into weeks and months, Mary could recall the words deliberately to mind, dwelling on them, measuring them, feeling a new illumination dawning in the once grim shadows of her mind.

In quiet Juttah and in the tranquility afforded her by Elizabeth's hospitality and counselling, she shaped the poetry that expresses the often recollected emotion. And she cannot help the exultation that begins her expression. 'My soul declares the greatness of the Lord. My spirit rejoices in God, my Saviour.'

Her whole being rejoices – 'My soul … and my spirit.' Her exuberance is palpable.

And is it any wonder?

'The Mighty One has done great things for me! Holy is his name.'

Her Saviour has looked, and has noted and marked, and radically changed the ' lowly condition of his servant.'

Her 'lowly condition' – to translate St Luke's word *tapeinosis* – does not mean 'humility,' but rather 'disgrace,' 'distress,' 'affliction,' 'degradation'. But her saviour, the Mighty One has done away with the shame. 'From now on, all generations will pronounce me blessed.'

The months of sorrow and fretting are gone. And the future, though it might hold pain and hardship, holds no more terror. The Mighty One will still do great things.

Mary measures what this 'Almightiness' means. She sees it in his age-long, unceasing lovingkindness and longsuffering mercy, lifting up the distressed and down-trodden, feeding the hungry and nurturing the deprived. She is heir to all the promises the God of Israel made to Isaac and Jacob, Moses, Joshua, David … and all her forefathers … since the days when Abraham, with God's promise, first came from Ur of the Chaldees to possess the land, and found the nation and people of the Hebrews.

As part of the solidarity of Israel, she is the recipient of God's promised mercy to her nation. Individual she may be but, as a member of Israel, she is, nevertheless, a beneficiary under God's

ancient and everlasting covenant with his people. 'This is the
heritage of the servants of the Lord, and their due reward from
me' (Is 54:17).

Israel's past is the promise for Mary's future.

And she raises her song in praise and thanks to God for the
personal mercies bestowed on her. This same song is bequeathed to us, an immortal anthem in which to offer unceasing
thanks to God for the mercies immeasurable he bestowed on us
in the birth of Jesus Christ.

Mary stayed with her about three months,
and returned home.

The sentence moves the story forward by glossing over details
and intimacies that St Luke considers of no pressing urgency or
importance in his record of Mary's stay with her cousin
Elizabeth. And he knows his readers will appreciate that the
journey she took from Nazareth to Juttah is the same journey she
must now undertake all the way back. And now, she is three
months longer pregnant.

But there's a nice human touch in St Luke's statement that's
easy to miss.

'She returned home,' he writes, or, as his own words have it,
'She returned to her own house.' He might have written, 'She returned to Nazareth.' But he doesn't. Instead, he writes that she
went 'to her own house'. To the house where Joseph her husband was, the house that was her home, and all that 'home'
means, bringing with her the hope and promise she would surely and sorely need to sustain her in the weeks and months and
years ahead.

CHAPTER SEVEN

Elizabeth's son
St Luke 1:57-80

Elizabeth's time came, and she bore a son.
Her neighbours and relatives heard
that the Lord had shown great mercy towards her,
and they shared her joy.
Then on the eighth day
they came to circumcise the child,
and they wanted to name him Zacharias,
after his father.
But his mother said, 'No, he is to be called John.'
They said to her,
'There is no one of your relatives
who is called by this name.'
They made signs to his father
as to what he wished him to be called.
He asked for a writing-tablet
and wrote, 'John is his name.'
All were astonished.
Immediately his mouth was opened
and his tongue loosed,
and he spoke, praising God.
Fear came upon all who lived in the neighbourhood,
and all these things were talked about
throughout the hill country of Judaea.
All who heard stored them in their minds, saying,
'What then will this child become?'
For indeed the hand of the Lord was with him.
His father Zacharias was filled with the Holy Spirit,
and prophesied, saying,
'Blessed is the God of Israel,

for he has visited his people and redeemed them.
He has raised up a strong Saviour for us
in the house of his servant David
(as he spoke through the mouth of the holy ones,
his prophets of long ago),
to save us from our enemies
and from the hand of all who hate us.
This was to show mercy towards our fathers,
and to remember his holy covenant,
an oath which he swore to our father Abraham
to grant us that,
being delivered from the hand of our enemies,
we should serve him unafraid
in holiness and righteousness before him all our days.
You too, child, will be called
a prophet of the Most High,
for you will go before the Lord to prepare his ways,
to give knowledge of salvation to his people
by the forgiveness of their sins
through the faithful compassion of our God,
by which the sunrise from on high will visit us,
to make its appearance to those who are sitting
in darkness and in the shadow of death,
in order to direct our feet into the way of peace.'

St Luke gives the impression that Elizabeth's 'time' came very soon after Mary had left. She was, as the angel revealed, six months pregnant at the time of his appearance to Mary. And Mary's visit lasted 'about three months'. The time, then, 'for Elizabeth to give birth was completed' not too long after Mary's departure.

'And she bore a son.' And it was the talk of the town. All the relatives gathered round, and the neighbours, delighted with the news. And glad that all had gone so well for the aged Elizabeth giving birth to a healthy young son. They brought joy and happiness, and shared the joy and rejoicing of the house.

St Luke, with sensitive simplicity, conveys the atmosphere of bustling joy and celebration. And his presentation suggests that he himself is enjoying writing up the episode. It's a family occasion, and he enters into it, reporting, with a kind of human relish, the goings-on in the house when all the relatives gather for the baby's circumcision and naming. 'Then on the eighth day, they came to circumcise the child,' he writes.

Circumcision was an ancient rite among the Hebrews. It was instituted in the time of Abraham. It was the sign of the Covenant which God made between himself and Abraham (Gen 17:1-14). The Covenant was made when Abraham was ninety-nine years old. As a sign of the Covenant, Abraham himself, like all the males in his household, was circumcised (Gen 17:24). It was an everlasting Covenant. The rite of circumcision, therefore, was an everlasting condition of the Covenant. And all male children were to be circumcised on the eighth day.

It was this rite, then, that Zacharias and his family, as descendants of Abraham, and heirs and beneficiaries of the Covenant, were now gathered to observe. And, at the same time, according to the custom, name their son. Had their child been a girl, she'd have been named after she was weaned.

The circumcision might be held in the synagogue or, if circumstances required, in the parents' house. St Luke's record gives the impression that the ceremony for Zacharias's son was conducted in the house.

The law directed that there be at least ten adults present, to form the *minyan, the number, the congregation,* to be witnesses.

Judging by the feel of St Luke's presentation, the priest's house is full. Filled, not just with relatives, but by neighbours in the little town, brimming with the pleasure of the birth of a son to Elizabeth. All in festive mood, but with the decorum suited to the solemnity of the occasion. There's serious work to be done. And careful surgery.

The room is set, the congregation forming itself around two chairs. One chair is for the *Sandak,* the 'godfather'. He will hold the baby boy on a cushion on his lap for the circumcision.

Nobody will sit in the second chair. It is 'Elijah's chair', since the prophet, the precursor of the Messiah, and patron of the rite of circumcision, was believed to be the unseen participant in the ceremony for which they were all gathered.

Amongst all those present are the secretary of the synagogue, a formal witness to the occasion, and the *Hazan*, the Reader of the synagogue who will conduct the ceremony. The *Mohel* (from the Hebrew word *mul*, to circumcise) is also present, to perform the rite of circumcision.

The Sandak took his place, sitting himself comfortably into his chair, settling the cushion carefully in his lap. Solemnity and excitement tingle the atmosphere. All eyes watch. The Sandak's wife carried in the baby boy, and placed him on the cushion. The Hazan and Zacharias and the Mohel follow. Elizabeth stood, discreetly, to the side.

There was no sound till the Hazan spoke.

'Blessed be God,' he began, 'who hath sanctified us by this commandment, and commanded us to enter our sons into the Covenant of Abraham.'

His prayer marked the beginning of the ceremony.

The Sandak held the boy with firm gentility while the Mohel stooped, and quickly, cleanly made the cut. He salved the incision with herbs and balms and powders till the blood was stanched, and made the uneasy boy as comfortable as he could on the cushion on the Sandak's lap.

The Hazan prayed the prayers that ended with a long 'Amen' in answer, and then led the whole company in reciting the Psalm, 'Blessed is every one who fears the Lord, and walks in his ways. You shall eat the fruit of your labours, you will be happy and prosperous ...' (Psalm 128).

The ceremony was ended. The Sandak's duties were finished. And he put the child in Elizabeth's comforting arms.

Then came the naming.

The relatives in acclamation named him 'Zacharias,' clapping and shouting with delight, congratulating the priest on producing a son in his old age.

'Not so,' rose Elizabeth's voice above the clamour. There was strength and determination in the sound. 'Not so.'

A shocked silence. Disbelief. The neighbours were surprised, Elizabeth's relatives were appalled. Elizabeth spoke quietly, 'He is to be called John.'

The house erupted. The solemn reverence that began the day's proceedings gone. The bright joviality that once named the child dulled, dimmed and disappeared.

And what was wrong with 'Zacharias' as a name? It was his father's name!

Every family has at least one relative who sees it as a solemn, moral duty to defend and uphold the family tradition. And, tight-faced, will castigate any other family member who dares to change or depart from it. And, especially, if it happens to be a mere 'in-law' who tries it on.

Elizabeth needed to be put in her place.

There was nobody in the entire family called John. And a chorus of voices reprimanded her, 'There is no one of your relatives who is called by this name.' Of course it was her privilege, as the boy's mother, to give him his name. But if she couldn't get it right, then his father would have to do it.

And the neighbours watched. A family row in the old priest's house! They had gossip that would last them a week!

The knowing ones of the family signalled to Zacharias, treating him as though he were deaf as well as dumb, insisting that he name his son.

But Zacharias was helpless. Unable to speak, he could only gesture in reply, shaping his hands, mouthing unsounding words. He wanted a tablet to write on.

They gave him a tablet, a slate coated with wax, and a stylus to write on it.

And they waited, tight-faced, purse-lipped, eyes burning smug confidence over well-trimmed beards, as Zacharias settled the tablet on his lap and took a strong hold on the stylus. This would put a stop to the upstart Elizabeth's presumption.

Zacharias wrote. A slow, strong, bold message in the wax. It

was crisp and short. Maybe it was the economy of a man communicating by writing. But it had about it more than a tinge of
determination, finality that would brook no contradiction.

The self-appointed chief of the knowing ones took the tablet
the old priest stretched out to him.

He read it. And paled. And he was hardly heard when he
whispered in disbelief, 'His name is John.'

Not a word was said. They marvelled all.

Zacharias stood up. And spoke. 'Blessed be the Lord God of
Israel,' he proclaimed as he made toward Elizabeth who was
nursing her child, 'for he has visited and redeemed his people.'

'Amen,' the houseful murmured, and said no more, rapt in
amazed attention at the old priest speaking.

'He has raised up a strong Saviour for us in the house of his
servant David,' the priest was saying, 'as he spoke through the
mouth of the holy ones, his prophets of long ago … to save us
from our enemies, and from the hand of all that hate us.'

Zacharias was talking into the awed silence. And his voice
was soft. But in it there was the sound of the urgency that nine
months of brooding and thinking and meditating had shaped
into his words. He was standing beside his wife as he was speaking. She was sitting in the Sandak's chair. It was comfortable and
easy for her as she nursed and comforted her baby son.

'This was to show mercy to our fathers,' the priest explained,
'and to remember his holy covenant. An oath which he swore to
our father Abraham.'

'Amen,' murmured the whisper from his listeners.

'To grant us that, delivered from the hand of our enemies, we
should serve him unafraid in holiness and righteousness before
him all our days.'

'Amen,' the houseful responded. And said no more as
Zacharias stooped and took his son from Elizabeth's arms.

'And you, my child,' he soothed, cradling his son to his bosom,
'will be called a prophet of the Most High.' He smoothed a gentle
hand across the forehead, and tucked the swaddling clothes more
snugly. 'You will go before the Lord to prepare his ways …'

The silence tensed at this prophecy by the priest. They were hearing from his own lips almost the very words which they'd been told the angel Gabriel had spoken to him as he served at the altar of incense in the Temple nine months ago. 'To give knowledge of salvation to his people by the forgiveness of their sins, through the faithful compassion of our God, by which the sunrise from on high will visit us ...'

'Amen,' every awe-struck hearer replied.

'To make its appearance to those who are sitting in darkness and in the shadow of death. In order to direct our feet into the way of peace.'

Zacharias stopped.

Nobody said anything.

They celebrated, but even the celebrations were quieter than they should have been.

The child grew and became strong in spirit. He was in the wilderness till the day of his presentation before Israel.

St Luke's note writes history with awesome economy. Thirty years of a man's life spanned and scanned in two sentences.

But, for the time being, as St Luke judges things, it's all we need to know about John, the son of Elizabeth and Zacharias.

CHAPTER EIGHT

The Birth
St Luke 2:1-7

In those days
a decree went out from Caesar Augustus
that all the world should be registered.
This registration was the first
when Quirinius was governor of Syria.

All went up to be registered,
each to his own city.

Joseph also went up from Galilee,
from the city of Nazareth, to Judaea,
to David's city which is called Bethlehem,
because he was of the house and family of David,
to be registered,
with Mary his betrothed, who was pregnant.

While they were there
her time came,
and she bore her first-born son;
and she wrapped him round
and laid him in a manger,
because there was no room for them
in the rest-house.

Mary was back in Nazareth. She was back in her own house, with Joseph, her husband. But, by the sound of things, she's no sooner settled-in than she's on the move again. This time, to Bethlehem. Facing the same long road all over again. But this time, it was with Joseph.

She went because Joseph went. And he went because he was

obliged to go, in obedience to a decree issued in Rome by Augustus Caesar, 'that all the world should be registered'.

'All the world,' as describing the Roman Empire at that time, was not an exaggeration. The Empire reached from Britain in the west, to Syria in the east; from Macedonia in the north, as far as Egypt in the south. It took in the whole sea-board of the Mediterranean.

Augustus was its emperor, the most powerful man in the world, ruling a vast and far-flung empire. And Augustus knew his empire. He had successfully commanded armies on the battlefields of most of it.

The shrewd, efficient Emperor, experienced in statecraft, understood the importance of knowing the population and resources of his empire. As a consequence, from time to time, he ordered a census to be taken in every province and kingdom of the Empire. The rulers and kings were in no position to object. They were appointees of the Emperor, and continued to rule only so long as he approved of them, and they paid him allegiance.

The census was the basis of the taxation system. And in the provinces and kingdoms outside Italy, it formed the basis on which he calculated the number of men he could levy on each as conscripts for the army that he deployed throughout the Empire.

Tribute, taxation, though, was the prime purpose of a census. The population of the Empire provided the revenue of the Empire.

There were two kinds of tax – a land tax (*tributum agri*) and a poll tax, a head tax (*tributum capitis*). Everybody, man, woman and even every slave, paid the poll tax. Land-owners paid both. The poll tax, the head tax, was the same for everybody. Men were liable from the age of fourteen, women from twelve. And they paid it until they were sixty-five.

The system spawned a new class known as *publicani*, tax-gatherers. In fact, they bought the right to collect tax. They were hated by the people of Palestine. Not only because they collected taxes for an occupying power, but also because of their extortion, and their callous, heartless treatment of those who could not meet their demands. They get a mention in the gospels. And Matthew, who later became an apostle of Jesus, is noted as a 'publican' in his office, collecting taxes, and keeping the list up-to-date (Matthew 9).

Methodical and meticulous Augustus paid serious and close attention to the statistics of the census. And, according to the Roman historian Tacitus, reporting in his *Annales*, the Emperor 'with his own hand' wrote a summary of the census, noting the citizens, and allies in arms, the kingdoms and provinces, their tributes and taxes.

During his reign as Emperor, Augustus ordered a universal census on three occasions. The second of these was about the time of the birth of Jesus. This is the census which St Luke has in mind when he writes, 'In those days a decree went out from Caesar Augustus that all the world should be taxed.'

In every other part of the Empire, the citizens registered in the place where they lived. In Judaea, however, things were organised differently. Judaea was part of Syria, a small, but fractious country at the far-flung reaches of the Empire. Already, Augustus had committed three legions of soldiers there to ensure order. At the southern tip of Syria was Judaea, a kingdom of people who smouldered with hatred for their Roman oppressors, and had a gut resentment of any kind of census or 'counting'.

History ruled their thinking. And this bit of history went far, far back to the days of king David.

David, it appears, took it into his head to have a census of the people. His army commander, Joab, advised against it. It would 'only bring guilt on Israel'. Obstinately. the king ignored the advice. Joab was directed to carry out the census. A plague afflicted Israel. In three days, seventy thousand people died. It was seen as God's displeasure at the king's presuming to count the people. Even Jerusalem looked liked being wiped out, till God stayed the hand of the destroying angel (see 1 Chron 21 and 2 Sam 24).

The episode lived in the memory of the nation. And Israelites lived with the belief that a 'counting' would cause the complete destruction of Palestine.

Augustus, if he knew about their sensitivities, was paying scant attention. He did, however, make an important concession, partly to avoid trouble from rebellious firebrands, but largely to save Herod, the king of Judaea, losing face amongst his own people. Instead of the census being conducted according to the Roman system, it followed the traditional Jewish custom of registering families in their ancestral districts.

The decree, then, had gone out, and 'all went up to be registered, each man (*ekastos*) to his own city.' Not, it might be said, in one fell swoop. The country didn't suddenly become a churning mass of men rushing to their birthplaces. The process took time, and was spread over a long period.

'Joseph also went up from Galilee, from the city of Nazareth, to Judaea, to David's city which is called Bethlehem, because he was of the house and family of David, to be registered ...'

It was the men who were required to attend. They registered, and gave details of their family and household, and whatever property and land they might own. There was no obligation on the women to attend. But Joseph went 'with Mary his betrothed, who was pregnant ' – or, as the AV measures the value of the word (*egkuos*) – 'great with child.'

Why did Joseph take Mary?

It could be one or both of two reasons. Mary and Joseph knew that the child to be born would be a boy. It doesn't need too great a stretch to imagine that Joseph, a Bethlehemite, himself born in David's city, should want the boy born there also. And was it in his mind, perhaps, to register the boy as his own son?

The more likely reason, though, seems to be that Joseph was deliberately taking Mary away to escape from the situation in Nazareth.

Things had little changed for her on her return from Juttah. She was no sooner back than the gossip-mongers began again where they had left off three months earlier. But, now, they were aggressive. It was no longer just the understandable crudeness and homespun prurience of earthy women with little experience and not too much imagination. Not any more. The early mockery had got out of hand. Now it was cruelty. Every look and word and comment was moulded, shaped and spiked to inflict hurt. And they succeeded.

The town that had given her life, had no pity for her while she nurtured her own child to birth.

It was a decision in Imperial Rome, where nobody was even aware of their existence, let alone their predicament, that gave Mary and Joseph the opportunity of escaping from Nazareth.

St Luke notices the occasion. 'A decree went out from Caesar Augustus that all the world should be registered.'

And it would be easy to feel that St Luke is deliberately setting out to relate the record he writes to the events of world history.

Maybe he was. But it's not his fine sense of history that matters here. What matters is his nice sense of Providence. What he notes, in fact, is the Providence that afforded the two people of whom he writes a solution to the difficulty that beset them. In obedience to the decree, Joseph goes to Bethlehem, 'with Mary his wife, who was great with child.'

It's not simply that he was taking Mary because he would not leave her behind in Nazareth in the prevailing conditions. His move is much more significant. He is cutting off all his ties with Nazareth. With Mary, he is leaving Nazareth for good, setting out to settle in Bethlehem, his native city.

That this was his intention is reflected in their action years later. When Herod was dead, they considered it safe to return to Palestine from their forced exile in Egypt. They would set out, not for Nazareth, but for Bethlehem.

They changed course and direction only because Archelaus had succeeded his father Herod, and now had jurisdiction over the area which included Bethlehem.

Mary, reports St Luke, 'was great with child.'

How great? There is no reason to suppose her pregnancy

didn't go to full term. The calculation, then, is straightforward. Mary conceived at or shortly after the angel's annunciation. She then 'made haste to go to Bethlehem'. Reckon that was a month after the annunciation. She stayed with Elizabeth three months. She then returned to Nazareth. Allow that she was in Nazareth a month or two before Joseph and herself set out for Bethlehem.

All of which means that, at the time they were travelling to Nazareth, Mary was five or six months pregnant. She arrived in Bethlehem five or six months pregnant.

The fact is worth bearing in mind.

St Luke goes on to write a careful and succinct account of the birth of Jesus.

But, for all the attention that's paid to him, the poor man needn't have bothered.

Time and tradition and sentimental piosity have shaped their own version of the circumstances of Jesus's birth, and littered the scene with caves and overcrowded inns and stables and cattle-stalls and sacred cows of all kinds.

Daring to suggest that things might have been different is to risk being accused of tampering with sacred truth. Of undermining what we have religiously misunderstood from the time we could first remember, and had our misconceptions reinforced by 'Once in royal David's city,' 'Away in a manger,' and a host of other songs and carols. They're all beautifully sentimental, but they misinterpret the evangelist's history of the event.

But perhaps it's worth daring the risk. It would go at least some of the way towards getting a clearer view of things. And, maybe, put right the misconceptions that are based on the tales and legends of the Apocryphal Gospels rather than the record which St Luke presents.

Take St Luke's account seriously, and there is no last-minute dash. No frantic father-to-be searching for a place in which his wife can give birth to her child. No over-crowded inns. No cattle-stalls, stables or lean-to sheds.

In St Luke's account, there is no room for the inn.

Indeed, the striking feature of the birth as St Luke presents it, in its Palestinian background, is its terrible ordinariness. It is a birth that looked no different from a birth in any other house in the land.

Writes St Luke, 'While they were there, the time for her to give birth was completed, and she bore her first-born son; and wrapped him round, and laid him in a manger, because there was no room for them in the inn.'

The key to getting things right lies in three statements in St Luke's account. And all three of them are contained in this single paragraph.

He begins, 'While they were there, the time came for her to give birth was completed.' There is no way he can state it more clearly. 'While they were there ...' Yet, this simple sentence is frequently overlooked. Ignored, even, in favour of a view that sees everything happening almost in panic, at the last minute.

'While they were there,' is the rendering of the Greek construction *en to einai*, implying *time during which*. It argues, not only that they were in Bethlehem, but that they were in Bethlehem long enough for Mary to wait and prepare herself for her pregnancy to come to term, and make the essential preparations for the birth of her child. She was still only six months pregnant.

St Luke doesn't mention where Mary and Joseph stayed, or with whom. He doesn't consider it's essential to the record. But, in a city that was Joseph's birthplace, it's not impossible to believe that he had relatives there. A family whose connections with the place went so far back in time might safely be assumed to have some, if not most of its members living there.

Joseph used the Tax Decree as the pretext for going to Bethlehem to settle there. He'd hardly go with no other advantage than that it was his native city. He went to Bethlehem because there he was sure of finding, if not bosom friends, at least close relatives.

The record as St Luke presents it, reflects more truly the character of Joseph painted by St Luke himself, and by St Matthew. A caring, loving. concerned husband, who would be unlikely to drag his wife along a journey of over one hundred miles, in the last stages of her pregnancy. He brought his wife to be amongst people who made her welcome.

And there the couple stayed, enjoying the hospitality, making new friends, renewing old acquaintances, relishing the kindness and comforting security. Until the day her promised child was born.

'She bore her first-born son,' St Luke writes, 'and wrapped him round, and laid him in the manger ...'

It is, perhaps, the mention of a manger that naturally conjures pictures of cattle-byres and stables as the scene for the birth.

But mangers were not exclusive to stables at the time of the birth of Jesus. They were, in fact, essential equipment in the ordinary Palestinian house.

The house itself was organised, more for sleeping than living in. And at night, the domestic animals were brought in, as much for safety as for shelter. And they shared the house with its human inhabitants. A manger held the food the animals might need in the night.

The scene St Luke describes so simply and directly, then, is nothing extraordinary. And, certainly, nothing like the background in which the prevailing popular fiction sets the birth.

Why did Mary place her newborn son in the manger?

But why not, in the circumstances? The delivery on the mat on the floor is completed, the child washed and cared for, the mother, after her ordeal, made comfortable. Now there is the inevitable tidying-up to do. Busy hands, and hurrying feet. Where better, then, for the infant, than the manger! Snug, safe, comfortable, and sleeping undisturbed. And yet, within arm's length of his mother, recovering from her ordeal, on the bedroll on the floor, near the still glowing brazier.

'She brought forth her firstborn son, and wrapped him in swaddling clothes, and laid him in the manger ...'

In this sentence, St Luke not only represents the simplicity and undramatic ordinariness of it all, but chooses language that communicates the atmosphere pervading the house – the pain and peril of childbirth, the frailty of the new-born child. And that phrase redolent with the caressing, protecting gentility of motherhood, 'and bedded him in the manger,' expressive enough as it sounds in English, but even more expressive, with the sound of poetry, in the language in which StLuke wrote it – *kai aneklinen auton en te phatne.*

'She brought forth her first-born son … and bedded him in the manger,' St Luke explains, 'because there was no room for them in the inn.'

It is here, perhaps, that the traditional tales of the birth most affect our reading and interpretation of St Luke's account.

Certainly, 'She laid him in a manger because there was no room for them in the inn,' is the statement that stands out boldly and insistently in any recollection of the birth narrative. And, on the English face of it, it all looks like stables and cattle-byres and over-crowded hotels.

The Apocryphal Gospels of the infancy offer stories of a cave and troublesome midwives; of Joseph, in his search for a mid-wife, meeting Eve who has come to see the fulfilment of the promise of redemption; of a child born in a *caravanserai* even before the midwife arrives.

What does St Luke mean when he writes, 'there was no room for them in the inn'?

To come at what St Luke is saying, it's best to begin by looking at a Palestinian house in the days of our Lord.

The ordinary Palestinian house was small, squarish, squat. It was not used for living in to the extent that we use ours. In Palestine's climate, there's no need to be indoors. The house was a place to sleep. A place which, at night, the family shared with the domestic animals. It was a rough and ready place with an earth floor, and the walls where jars and pots of various kinds were ranged.

There were two levels to the ground floor. The door of the house led into one level. The domestic animals were kept here at night. On the side opposite the door, there was a low wall that rose to the next level. This was the family area. At one end of the wall, a few steps gave access to the family space. And, on the low wall, there was fixed the manger.

Up one of the outside walls, there ran a flight of steps to a flat, parapetted roof. On the roof, when it was necessary, there was erected a booth or tent which, in this ordinary home, served as a guest-chamber. In a richer house this guest-chamber would be a more permanent extra storey.

The Greek word for this 'guest-chamber' is *kataluma*.

And this is the word St Luke uses when he writes his account of the birth. 'There was no room for them in the *kataluma*.'

The Old Testament details two instances of ordinary people providing such a 'guest-chamber'. The prophet Elijah lived in a roof-chamber provided for him by the widow in Zarephath (1 Kgs 17:19). A man and his wife in Shunem built a roof-chamber for the prophet Elisha. And the passage explains what the room contained. 'Let us make for him an upper-chamber, a small place, and let us put there for him a bed, a table, a stool and a candlestick' (2 Kgs 4:10).

St Luke is noted for the care he takes in choosing the right word to say what he wants to say. So that here he can be expected to choose his language just as carefully.

That *kataluma* cannot mean 'inn' in the 'hotel' sense, is borne out by St Luke's deliberate choice of a different word when he's recording the Parable of the Good Samaritan (10:34, 35). In the parable, he uses *pandocheion, an inn*, in the proper sense. And he repeats the idea by using the word *pandochei* to identify the innkeeper.

Not alone does he use *kataluma* in his birth account, he uses it again in chapter 22:11. There it is used to describe the place where Jesus had the Last Supper with his apostles. St Mark, also, uses *kataluma* in writing of the place of the Last Supper.

All in all, the word *kataluma* occurs only three times in the gospels – once in St Mark, and twice in St Luke.

The English versions have no difficulty in rendering it 'guest-chamber' in connection with the Last Supper. And this 'guest-chamber,' according to St Mark and St Luke, was an 'upper room' in a private house.

It would seem, then, that St Luke is aware of the connotation of the word he uses. So that, if he uses the word in one place with a precise meaning, it seems a bit whimsical to give it an altogether different meaning in the other.

If *kataluma* connotes a guest-chamber on the upper storey of a private house for the Last Supper, it's hardly on to make it mean a public inn, a *khan*, a *caravanserai*, when the evangelist uses it in his record of the birth.

What St.Luke is writing about, then, is the guest-chamber on the roof of this house in Bethlehem, in which, for one reason or another, there was no place for them to lie down.

And what could possibly be the reason?

It may be that the weather, while not bad enough to prevent the robust sleeping there, was not good enough for a woman giving birth to her child.

There may be a different reason, if we follow one old commentator who suggested that Jesus was born in the month of Nisan (March-April), the month of Passover. If this is correct, then it might well be that the guest-chamber, like the rest of the house, was already occupied with relatives home to celebrate the Feast.

There is, however, a somewhat simpler and more obvious reason. It depends, though, on precisely who it is St Luke means when he writes that there was no room *for them*.

Bearing in mind that, in this particular paragraph, he focuses attention on Mary and her newborn son. He writes, 'She brought forth her firstborn son, wrapped him in swaddling clothes, and bedded him in the manger, because there was no place for them in the guest-chamber.' It seems correct, then, to decide that he does not mean Mary and Joseph, nor even Mary, Joseph and the child, but simply Mary herself and her newly-born child. There was no place for Mary and her new-born son in the guest-chamber.

And, in this case, it could well be that there was no place in the guest-chamber on the roof, because it was already occupied by the men of the house who, for privacy's sake, were keeping out of the way, affording Mary and her helping women the privacy properly belonging to a woman in childbirth.

Mary, then, not occupying the guest-room, gave birth to Jesus on the ground-floor of the house in Bethlehem.

The record St Luke writes is simple, simple, simple. Uncluttered, uncomplicated. Human. Eloquently ordinary. The account of a young woman bearing the gruelling labour to bring her son to birth. In a house in Bethlehem.

It's a pity that it has all been thrown away and lost, in favour of a story based on a careless reading of St Luke's careful record.

We owe the man a huge debt.

St John may proclaim in banner headlines, 'The Word was made flesh.' St Luke brings us as close to the scene as dignity and human courtesy and sensitivity will permit. His plain, straightforward telling affords us the privilege of being glimpsing witnesses of the Incarnation.

CHAPTER NINE

The Shepherds
St Luke 2:8-20

*In the same district
shepherds were living out in the fields,
and keeping the night watches over their flock.*

*An angel of the Lord came upon them,
and the glory of the Lord shone round them,
and they were greatly afraid.*

*The angel said to them,
'Do not be afraid, I proclaim to you a great joy,
which will be for all the people:
today a Saviour who is the Anointed Lord
has been born for you in the city of David.*

*This is the sign for you:
you will find a baby, wrapped round
and lying in a manger.'*

*Suddenly a great company of the heavenly army
was with the angel,
praising God and saying,
'Glory in the highest to God,
on earth peace among men of his choice!'*

*When the angels had departed from them into heaven,
the shepherds said to one another,
'So let us go over to Bethlehem
and see this thing that has happened,
which the Lord has made known to us.'*

They hurried and came,
and they found Mary and Joseph,
and the baby lying in the manger.

When they saw
they made known what had been told them about this child.
All who heard it were astonished at what was told them
by the shepherds,
but Mary preserved all these things,
pondering them in her mind.

And the shepherds returned,
giving glory to God and praising him
for all that they had heard
and seen as it had been told them.

Read what St Luke has written. Read it aloud. But read it from the shepherds' point of view, for that's how St Luke writes it.

He has entered into the mind of the shepherds. He's one of them. It's as though he were there in the field with them. He sees what they see. He hears what they hear. He responds and reacts as they do. This is the gentle, sensitive Luke bursting with excitement and enthusiasm. And, all the while, trying to stay calm enough to present an orderly report.

And what a task he has!

This is not just the announcement to a few men in a field about the birth of a boy in Bethlehem, coupled with brief suggestions on how to recognise him. The event St Luke is describing, is unique in scripture. Nowhere in scripture is any event heralded in such majesty and splendid brilliance. The giving of the law, by comparison, was a quiet occasion, the crossing at the Red Sea almost a non-event.

'In the same district shepherds were living out in the fields, and keeping the night watches over their flocks. An angel of the Lord came upon them, and the glory of the Lord shone round them, and they were greatly afraid.'

So St Luke begins to describe the event, entering into his record the appearance of yet another angel.

But this time, there is a difference.

When he wrote about the appearance of the angel to Zacharias and to Mary, all he said was that each angel had been sent. Now, though, not only does he write that the 'angel of the Lord came upon them,' but goes on to add, 'and the glory of the Lord shone round them.'

In all the New Testament, St Luke is the only writer who uses this precise combination of words – *'the glory of the Lord,' he doxa kuriou*. It is, though, a common enough expression in the Greek version of the Old Testament, the Septuagint. It is used as a rendering of the Hebrew expression *k'bodh Jehovah, the glory of God*. It conveys the idea of the shining forth of light by which God's presence is recognised by men.

The idea of 'the glory of God', is rooted deep in Israel's religion. It goes back to the earliest days of the Old Testament, and the incident of Moses's meeting Jehovah, and the hewing out of the Ten Commandments (Ex 33:17-23).

It's this background that shapes and colours St Luke's thinking as he writes about the shepherds. He lifts the words 'the glory of the Lord', *he doxa kuriou* complete and intact from the Septuagint version, to explain how things are with the shepherds. They are faced, not simply with a messenger sent from God but are, unmistakably, in the presence of God himself. The angelic visitor is the mouthpiece. The surrounding 'glory of the Lord' is the physical appearance that indicates the presence of God.

What exactly they saw in the new light of the breaking dawn, or how they felt the presence, St Luke does not explain. Is it possible to explain? All that he can write is that 'an angel of the Lord came upon them, and the glory of the Lord shone round them.'

'They were greatly afraid,' he explains. Of course they were. They were startled and frightened. But St Luke's own expression 'they feared with a great fear', suggests more than just their immediate and natural reaction to the phenomenon. It carries in it the feel of their reverential fear, their religious response, their awe in the presence of an awe-inspiring God.

But their fear also had another side. The shepherds were reared on the Old Testament. They know, then, that the appearance of God's 'glory' was a sign either of divine favour (Lev 9:6, 23) or, more frequently, divine anger (Ex 16:7; Num 14:10). And, by the sound of things, they expected a word of reprimand.

But, they are given, instead, a word of assurance. 'Do not be afraid. I proclaim to you a great joy ...' The 'glory of the Lord' is revealed. The Lord speaks through his messenger. And the word is a word of promise. 'A great joy which will be for all the people.'

The episode St Luke is presenting would not be out of place in the Old Testament.

The angel makes no delay in proclaiming what the good news, the great joy is. 'Today a Saviour who is Christ the Lord has been born to you in the city of David.'

That has to be one of the most auspicious and exhilarating statements of history. Yet, nowadays, it's easy to read, or even listen to it being dramatically read, and still be unmoved by it. Part of the reason lies in the fact that it is familiar stuff. We have grown so accustomed to it that its often repetition has dulled our responses. We come to it with the cumulative experience of two thousand years of living with it.

But stand where the shepherds stand. The shepherds hear it as members of a race that for almost a thousand years have waited for this very message.

A thousand years of messianic hope, a hope which had begun as a thought that eased itself into the mind of the people in the dereliction which overtook the nation after the days of David and Solomon (922BC). A nostalgia for the good old days, but a sentiment that shaped and turned itself into a hope. A religious longing that the day would come in the nation when Jehovah, in keeping with his Covenant with David, would restore the greatness that once was Israel. A hope which some generations saw crescendo to a climax, and others saw dashed and almost lost. But still a burning hope that waxed and waned through the long centuries, bolstering, urging, inspiring the nation to keep alive.

A thousand years of waiting. But now, at last, everything was there. The message is that Jehovah's ancient promise to the nation is fulfilled.

It hardly needs the refined mind and emotions of a poet to imagine how the shepherds felt, and reacted to this stupendous announcement.

Measure the significance of this fleeting moment in the interminable history of Israel, as the shepherds must have measured it, and it's no longer a surprise that St Luke takes such pains to establish the atmosphere in which the message is delivered. And who it is who delivers it.

Such a declaration of such a fulfilment of a so long cherished hope could be made, dared be made, only by God himself.

No wonder the evangelist is careful to report that, 'the glory of the Lord shone round them'!

Israel as a nation, of course, was accustomed to the coming and going of saviours, raised up by God to meet particular situations. While the news, then, would certainly excite the shepherds and the nation, it's hardly enough to warrant God himself revealing himself in such slendour and majesty to announce it.

But the Shepherds know the reason. They're listening to what the messenger is saying. This Saviour is born 'in the city of David.' That's good. Born 'in the city of David,' this deliverer can only be The Messiah.

Which is exactly how the angel describes him. He is the Christ, *Christos*.

Christos is the word the Septuagint uses to translate the Hebrew word *mashiah*, anointed one. In different forms the word is used in the Old Testament of kings, of the Patriarchs. Above all, though, it is used of the appointment of the offspring of David, through whom God would rule over his people. Connecting this deliverer, then, with David's city, means that he is *The* Messiah.

That's better. But the best they have yet to hear. This Saviour is Christ the Lord, *Christos Kurios*.

Kurios is the word frequently used to render the Hebrew word *Adonai*, Lord, the usual substitute for the name Jehovah.

To the Jewish ears and the Jewish minds of the shepherds, *Christos Kurios*, Christ the Lord, can mean only one thing. Never was there news like this news! And they would not be surprised were the hosts of heaven to burst into rejoicing and singing praise to God. Never was a promise so amply fulfilled! Pressed down, shaken together, and running over, has God poured into Israel's bosom!

For now, it is no longer simply a matter of God sending a Saviour, a Messiah into the world. *Christos Kurios* means nothing less than that God himself has come as Messiah.

But could the shepherds believe this? Could they be sure that it had happened?

'This is the sign for you …' the angelic messenger assures them.

The word sign, in Greek *semeion*, echoes the Old Testament word *Oth*, a sign, a kind of fingerpost (Jdgs 6:17), a token of God's faithfulness to his promise (2 Kgs 20:8, 9).

What is happening will set their wondering at rest. The event, which is the very content of these good tidings, is the sign and seal of God's continued mercy and lovingkindness towards his people, the token that he has not forgotten his covenant. And the token that The Messiah has come is a babe, born in Bethlehem. 'This is the sign for you. You will find a babe, wrapped in swaddling clothes, lying in the manger.'

It's almost established – and, by implication, incontrovertible – tradition to interpret 'this is the sign for you', as meaning no more and no less than 'this is how you will recognise him.'

But this is to misunderstand the biblical conception of a sign. It also ignores the later comment by Simeon in the Temple – 'This child is set for a sign that shall be spoken against,' – which makes it too plain that the sign in question is Jesus, the child Jesus. The 'wrapped in swaddling clothes, and lying in the manger,' is not offered as an additional hint for easy recognition. It has nothing to do with stressing the circumstances which will make the baby instantly identifable. It is, rather, a way of emphasising the new-bornness of the babe.

The newborn babe in Bethlehem is the sign and token of God's faithfulness to his word; the focal point at which God's continuous activity becomes plainly manifest to men; the means by which God testifies to mankind of his goodness.

'Suddenly,' writes St Luke, as though he would startle his readers every bit as much as the Shepherds themselves were startled.

The angel is still there. Is he advising them where to search in Bethlehem? Telling them, perhaps, who the parents are, and where they're living?

The shepherds are in a huddle, dazed, amazed, still in shock, trying to come to terms with what has happened and what they've heard from the angel.

'And suddenly! With the angel was a great company of the heavenly army, praising God.'

Stay with the Shepherds. Stay in the field, and feel the exhilaration, the joy, the cloud-bursting rejoicing.

What St Luke is writing is not just a dramatic ending to an already sufficiently imaginative piece of writing. He's trying to describe a scene that is unique. Never in scripture was any event heralded in such a display of majesty, might, and dazzling splendour. A new age has begun for mankind. It is the promise of 'The Lord of Hosts' (Micah 4:4). And the evangelist is at pains to establish that it is being spoken now by the Lord of Hosts, Jehovah Sabbaoth , surrounded by all the panoply of heaven.

If God's presence is at first revealed to the shepherds by the 'glory' that shone round them, that presence is now doubly authenticated by the arrival of *The Heavenly Host, S'ba hashamayim*. The heavens are open. The might, majesty and glory of God is revealed. And the multitude of the 'Heavenly Host' attend to witness the occasion.

And this uniqueness, surely, accounts for the exhilaration that issues in the angels' hymn, praising and blessing God, telling out his lovingkindness to mankind.

The angelic messenger who brought the glad tidings in the first place, feels the joy himself. And his song, in which the whole company of heaven joins, is the expression of joyous hearts. The song itself, with its three clauses, forming a Hebrew parallelism, is a piece of poetry in the best Hebrew tradition:

'Glory in the highest to God,

On earth peace ... to men of his choice.'

The message delivered, the praises sung, the angels disappear as suddenly as they had come. And the Shepherds are left. The sky is quiet again, and in the quick-rising dawn, the only sound comes from bleating sheep in the folds.

'When the angels had departed from them into heaven,' St Luke reports, 'the shepherds said to one another, "So let us go over to Bethlehem, and see this thing that has happened, which the Lord has made known to us".'

It was a spontaneous reaction by the shepherds. That's the impression St Luke's account gives. It's as though each man said, in unison almost, with his companions, 'Let us go ...'

And small wonder. What they were going to see was what 'the *Lord* had made known' to them. Not the angelic messenger. He was merely the echo of the voice of God. They were going to see what God himself had made known to them. The shepherds would not mouth the divine name but, as reverential Jews, spoke of him as *Adonai , the Lord* ... 'What the Lord has made known to us.' God had spoken.

And the shepherds are going to Bethlehem to see the reality of this promise, the substantiation of the word which, amid all the majesty and panoply of heaven 'the Lord has made known' to them.

There's a depth of meaning in the statement the evangelist attributes to the shepherds which is lost in the normally anaemic English translations. St Luke's sentence is stronger and much more significant than the usual, 'and see this thing which is come to pass.'

Read more carefully what St Luke actually writes, and what he says is, 'and see this word which is come into being'. The term he uses is *hrema*, word. And *hrema* can never – or should never – be translated to mean 'thing'. It means 'word', in the same way that *logos* means 'word'.

St Luke is not given to banner headlines or soundbites as St John is. But he's saying exactly the same thing. If St John proclaims 'The word was made flesh', St Luke is saying no less. 'Let us see this word which is come into being.'

St Luke has the shepherds saying, 'this *word* which has come into being.' He's writing about the Incarnation, the Word made flesh. And in the most telling manner in the New Testament. Where St John is content to state the fact in a soundbite, St Luke presents the fact happening. And his presentation could not be more intimate, vivid and dramatic. God speaks the word.

'Let us go ... and see this word which has come into being,' is the shepherds' response. 'And they came ... and found the babe ...'

How far is it to Bethlehem.

'Not very far,' is the assurance in the song. And tourists are comforted with having the 'Shepherds' Field' within reasonable walking distance of the alleged place of the birth.

'Let us go now even unto Bethlehem' is how the Authorised Version translates St Luke's account of what the shepherds decided. And the impression is that the shepherds, despite the distance involved, were still prepared to go all the way to Bethlehem. Being in the same 'district' does nothing to shorten their journey. St Luke's *chora* means district, of course. But it also mean 'a region, a great geographical division of a province'. The Authorised Version translates the word as 'country.'

The Shepherds, then, might have been anywhere in Judaea and, consequently, faced several days' travelling to reach Bethlehem.

It may not affect the issue one way or the other, but it's still worth having in mind, that the only other journey St Luke notes as having been made 'with haste' is Mary's journey to Elizabeth. That was a distance of some one hundred and thirty miles.

At any rate, there's a need to be cautious in settling too easily for a quick sprint by the shepherds across a few neighbouring fields.

'They came,' reports St Luke, 'and found Mary and Joseph. And the babe lying in the manger.'

The stark, simple ordinariness of St Luke's statement conveys the utter ordinariness of the scene that greeted the shepherds. It was a setting they might have found after a birth in any ordinary house in the land.

And, if ever the ordinariness of Jewish life had divine significance, it had it now. And it may not be totally insignificant that the men to whom the birth was so dramatically announced, and who now witnessed the reality of that proclamation, were amongst the despised of Israel. There was a saying in those days, attributed to Rabbi Gorion, 'Let no man make his son a muleteer, a camel-driver, a barber, a sailor, a shepherd, an innkeeper, forasmuch as their craft is a craft of robbers.'

St Luke goes on, 'When they saw, they made known what had been told them about this child.' How succinctly the evangelist sums things! He's writing about a bunch of men in from the fields, who've seen and heard things no man had ever heard or seen before. Their clothes still reek of the smell of the sheep they live amongst and shepherd. They're standing, heaped into a small space, already full enough with people. But they hardly notice them, oblivious of the upheaval and inconvenience their sudden and unexpected arrival might have caused in the house.

The birthing is over. Some time ago, by the tidy look of things. So, at least, they're not interrupting that. They're looking ... Exhilaration chasing disbelief, excitement smothering wonder ... It could be that there wasn't another soul in the house, for they didn't see them. They see only what they came to find. Mary and Joseph. And the babe lying in the manger ... And they're seeing it all exactly as the heavenly messenger had told them they'd see it ...

They can contain themslves no longer. They burst out ... everyone all at once. Talking, talking, till they sound almost gabby ... the angel ... the message ... today a Saviour has been born ... you will find a babe ... the sign that Messiah is come ... the heavens bursting with the sight and sound of the hosts of heaven praising God ...

And, then, it's as though St Luke would calm things a bit. He writes simply, soberly, quietly. 'All they who heard were amazed at what was told them by the shepherds.' They couldn't be anything else.

But who were 'all they' who were amazed? Joseph's relatives whose house Mary and himself had shared over the past few months? The helping women who'd tended and talked and coaxed and encouraged Mary through the birth of her child. And had told her she'd brought forth a son? Neighbours who'd called to congratulate her ... and, maybe, just a little bit out of noseyness? And did the 'all they' include those who, up to now, had kept out of the way in the guest-chamber, leaving no space there for Mary and her newborn son?

'All they', whoever they were, stayed with the Holy Family after the shepherds had left.

All of which paints the picture of a rather fuller, busier, and more homely company than the one associated with the loneliness of the cave or stable we are, mistakenly, encouraged to believe.

The shepherds' delight, it would seem, was nothing lessened by the time they were leaving. 'The shepherds returned,' writes St Luke, 'giving glory to God, and praising him for all they had heard and seen as it had been told them.' And, no doubt, their rollicking joy and noisy praises causing a bit of commotion in the quiet neighbourhood.

But, in the middle of all the amazement and praise, Mary does not speak. She listens and hears. After the ordeal of the birth, she's in no great mood for asking questions or expressing an opinion. Her newborn son is warmly wrapped and safely sleeps, cosily bedded in the manger. And she rests comfortably on her bed-roll. But she misses nothing. And, as St Luke notices, 'Mary kept all their words, and pondered them in her mind.' Going over in her mind all the events of the last months, perhaps? Remembering, recollecting, hearing all over again, the angel Gabriel's message all those months ago, 'you will bear a son ... He will be great. He will be called Son of the Most High ...'

CHAPTER TEN

The Wise Men
St Matthew 2:1-12

When Jesus was born in Bethlehem of Judaea
in the time of King Herod,
Magi from the east came to Jerusalem,
saying, 'Where is the new-born King of the Jews?
For we have seen his star at its rising,
and have come to worship him.'

Hearing this, King Herod was troubled
and all Jerusalem with him.

And when he had brought together
all the chief priests and scribes of the people,
he asked them where the Messiah was to be born.

They said to him, 'In Bethlehem of Judaea;
for it is written thus through the prophet:
Thou, Bethlehem in the land of Judah,
art by no means least among the rulers of Judah,
for out of thee a leader shall come
who shall rule my people, Israel.'

Then Herod, having secretly called the Magi,
tried to learn precisely from them
the time when the star appeared,
and sent them to Bethlehem,
saying, 'Go and make exact enquiries about the child,
and when you find him, bring me word,
that I too may come and worship him.'

Having heard the king, they departed,
and the star which they saw at its rising went before them,
till it came and stopped over the place where the child was.

When they saw the star,
they rejoiced very greatly.

And when they had entered the house
they saw the child with his mother Mary.

They fell and worshipped him.
And, opening their caskets,
they offered to him gifts,
gold and frankincense and myrrh.

Being instructed in a dream
not to go back to Herod,
they withdrew to their own country by another road.

When St Matthew writes his account of the visit of the Wise Men, the Magi, he writes history in short sentences.

He writes of the Wise Men's coming, their obeisance, their gifts. He explains, in clipped statements, about their movements and their changing the route of their return journey to their homeland. He writes about the flight of the holy family, and their eventual return to live in Nazareth.

But brief and sketchy as all the reports are, they hide in their curtness, a welter of background information, and insight into the conditions of the time. Through it all, he conveys the feeling of the messianic hope that had been so long prevalent and was now growing in intensity. He reflects the political intrigue which had shaped the reign of Herod the king for almost forty years. The same intrigue that still affected the king's thinking and his conduct. He affords glimpses of conditions in Israel at the death of Herod, and the subsequent accession of his son Archelaus.

But, before becoming too involved in all that, a few obvious questions: Who were the Wise Men? How many were there, and where did they come from? What about the star? When did they pay homage?

Who were the Wise Men?

St Matthew's own word for them as a group is *Magoi*, which, by way of the Latin translation, gives the word *Magi*, to describe them.

They were magicians, astromoners, astrologers. The term Magi originally referred to a priestly caste amongst the Medes and Persians who concerned themselves with physics, medicine and astrology. In Old Testament times, they were known as Chaldeans, Babylonians. In their own day, and amongst their own people, they were the intelligentia, the philosophers, held in honour and esteem.

They searched into nature, especially into the movement and motion of the planets.

There were, they reckoned, seven planets – the Moon, the Sun, Mercury, Venus, Saturn, Jupiter and Mars. In the eastern sky, they counted twelve stars, and twelve also in the west. The stars, they taught, could augur good times and bad times, happiness and suffering, justice, wars, peace … anything that could happen, good, bad or indifferent. The conjunctions of the planets, they considered, were especially important in the affairs of individuals and nations alike.

The Jews themslves, of course, were involved in astrology. They, too, cast horoscopes, convinced that the stars had influence over the fates and fortunes of people, high and low. 'Life, children, and a livelihood depend not on merit, but on the influence of the stars,' declares the Talmud. 'The influence of the stars makes wise, the influence of the stars makes rich.'

The Jewish historian Josephus cites Berosus, a Babylonian priest-writer around 260 BC, who describes Abram as 'a man righteous and great … and skilful in the celestial science.'

The priestly caste of the Magi was, reputedly founded by Baalam. Baalam himself is presented in the Old Testament as a cult priest (Num 22-24). He lived in Babylon, at Pethor on the Euphrates. He practised augury and divination, and had a reputation for casting spells that worked – 'whom you bless is blessed; whom you curse is cursed.' (Num 22:6).

He has a place in the history of Israel because he was sum-moned – and paid – by Balak, king of Moab, to come and curse the Israelites swarming through Moab on their journey from Sinai to the Promised Land, and threatening to eat Moab out of house and home.

Instead of cursing the Israelites, however, Baalam blessed them. And, in the process, forecast that 'a star will come forth out of Jacob, a comet will arise from Israel' (Num 24:17).

Centuries later, Baalam's forecast was seen as a prophecy about the star that would appear at the time of Jesus's birth.

The Magi of whom St Matthew writes, and the rest of their priestly caste, were successors in the practice of astrology that was something of a science. And they were masters of their art. They were depended on for direction, prediction, and advice. They were the counsellors, the judges, the oracles of the East.

'Wise Men' is an apt and appropriate title for these men who arrived, seeking the 'new-born King of the Jews'.

How many were there, and where did they come from?
There is no way of knowing how many Wise Men arrived to pay homage to the new-born King of the Jews.

St Matthew obviously doesn't think it necessary to mention the number. Any more than St Luke feels it incumbent on him to say how many shepherds there were. And nobody seems greatly concerned about filling the gap St Luke leaves!

However, because St Matthew reports that the Magi present-ed gold and frankincense and myrrh – three gifts – it is popularly assumed that there were only three men.

Calculating the number of men on the basis of the number of gifts mentioned, seems reasonable enough. It could, of course, also be a mistake. The fact that a man, retiring after long service with his firm, is presented with a cheque and a gold watch, doesn't necessarily mean that only two people attended the farewell party.

St Chrysostom of Antioch, and St Augustine, one of the four Latin Doctors of the Church, both dismiss the idea of there being

only three. Writing in about AD400, they suggest twelve Wise
Men, representing the twelve tribes of Israel. Three hundred
years later, the English scholar-monk, Bede – or the venerable
Bede, as he was known – settled for three. And he names them,
Melchior, Caspar and Balthasar. His spelling differs only slightly
from the spelling in the apocryphal Armenian *Gospel of the Infancy*.

This book, which purports to have been written by St James,
the Lord's brother, gives the names as Melkon, Gaspar and
Balthasar. The same book tells that they brought as a gift the
testament which Adam gave to his son Seth, the son Adam reckoned God had sent to replace his son Abel whom Cain had murdered.

The Venerable Bede explains what each man looked like, and
the gift he presented. Melchior was an old man with white hair
and a sweeping beard. He presented the gold. Caspar, who offered the frankincense, was a beardless, ruddy youth. The man
who gave the myrrh was Balthasar, a swarthy man, in the prime
of life.

And they were all kings, it appears. From Persia, India and
Arabia. For kings, it might be said, they seem to have got a pro-
nouncedly low-key reception at the house in Bethlehem.
Though, by the sound of things, they didn't leave the house entirely empty-handed. The Arabic *Gosepl of the Infancy* carries the
information that the Wise Men brought home one of Jesus's
swaddling cloths, which was fireproof.

Babylon, of course, is not out of the question as one of the
places from which the Magi might have come. Near the city of
Babylon, and not far from Abraham's old city, Ur, was the town
called Sippar. There was a school of astrology at Sippar. And the
town was not more than four or five months' travel, about eight
hundred miles, from Jerusalem.

What about the star?
Comets and the conjunction of planets, close enough to appear
in the heavens as a 'star', was not new thinking at the time of
Jesus's birth. And such conjunctions were believed to herald the

birth of great leaders. There was a tradition amongst Jews that Moses was born three years after the conjunction of the planets Jupiter and Saturn in the constellation of 'The Fish', Pisces.

The ancient prophecy of Baalam told that a great star would appear to herald the coming of the Messiah (Num 24:17). This was firmly believed by the Jews. And their forced exile, their captivity, in Babylon by Nebuchadnezzar spread the belief in the East. The Magi knew about it. If not from the Jews, then, as heirs and successors of Balaam, the reputed founder of the caste.

Whatever we know by way of explaining the 'star' at the birth of Jesus, we know, mainly as the result of the researches by Johannes Kepler.

Kepler became Astronomer Royal in Prague, at the Court of Rudolf II in 1601. In 1603, he observed and described a conjunction of the two planets Jupiter and Saturn. So close a conjunction as to appear as one star. It took place in the constellation Pisces. Kepler calculated backwards and discovered that the same kind of conjunction had appeared in May, October and December of 7 BC, just about the time of the birth of Jesus.

Kepler's work was lost and forgotten for about two hundred years, but was rediscovered in the eighteen hundreds.

The results of his researches, however, were confirmed in 1925. A German scholar named Schnabel deciphered a cuneiform inscription (written in wedge-shaped or arrow-shaped figures) which had been made at the school of astrology in Sippar, in Babylon. This showed calculations of the planets in 7 BC, as indeed Kepler himself had calculated.

In Jewish tradition, Pisces was reckoned the sign of Israel, if not, indeed, of the Messiah. Saturn was considered Israel's guardian star. And Jupiter, besides being the star of good fortune, was also the star of a king. The conjunction of Jupiter and Saturn in the constellation Pisces, the Magi would interpret as meaning that a new king, the Messiah, was to be born in Israel.

It may not be the 'yea' or 'nay' of the argument. But it goes a deal of the way in making sense of St Matthew's account of the Magi, and the 'star' which they saw.

When did the Magi come to pay homage?

The traditional answer is that the Magi arrived some longish time after the birth. It might have been six or eight days. It might have been two years.

The idea that it was six days or eight days, stems from the assumption that Jesus was born in a cave. The apocryphal story is that Mary and Joseph stayed in the cave with their new-born child for three days. Then they moved to a stable. The child was laid in the manger, and the ox and the ass adored him. They stayed in the stable for another three days. And then, they moved to a house in Bethlehem. So, they were established in a house when the Wise Men arrived.

All of which suits the speculation to St Matthew's account of the Magi's visit, 'When they had entered the house, they saw the child ...' It is speculation. But speculation that has little real foundation, and is hard to take. Especially in view of St Luke's clear-cut account of Jesus having been born in a house in the first place.

The 'two years after' idea rests on St Matthew's note that Herod 'sent and killed all the boys ... who were two years old and under.' It looks promising enough as a beginning. But it misses the point of Herod's age-range. And it ignores other statements in St Matthew's account.

In the days when Jesus was born, mothers suckled their babies for about two years. Girls were weaned after a year, boys after two years. Herod's intention was that not a single male infant in Bethlehem should be left alive. His plan, then, with his 'two years old and under' directive, was to cover all eventualities, and to be sure of hitting the right target. It can hardly be used, then, to establish that the Magi arrived two years after the birth.

Indeed, there's enough in St Matthew's account to suggest that, not only did the Magi arrive on the day of the birth, but may, in fact, have paid their homage even before the shepherds.

The Magi, after all, came looking for a 'new-born King'. It's not unreasonable, then, to conclude that they were searching for a newly-born child, and not a two-year old infant. The point of the 'star', surely, is that from it the astrologers forecast the day of the birth. It's highly unlikely that they'd got their calculations so wrong that they arrived two years after the birth. And at a time when the King they had come to worship could no longer be described as new-born.

What they found was 'the child'. The word St Matthew uses to describe the child, *paidion*, is exactly the same word as St Luke uses to describe the child, *paidion*, of whom the Shepherds spoke (Lk 2:17).

But what the shepherds actually saw, as St Luke makes clear, was the baby, *brephos*. Yet, within a few breaths of seeing the baby, the shepherds are talking about 'this child'. This has to mean that either the shepherds' 'baby' had quickly grown old enough to be a 'child', or else the 'child' the Magi saw was equally a 'baby'.

There is no problem about accepting that the shepherds arrived at the house in next-to-no-time after the birth. And certainly on the same day. Does there have to be a problem, then, about the Magi also arriving on the same day?

But bear the argument a bit longer. And go a bit further in this comparison between what the Wise Men saw and what the Shepherds saw.

The scene for the Shepherds was 'Mary and Joseph. And the baby lying in the manger.' What the Wise Men saw was 'the child with his mother Mary'.

At least one commentator suggests that the Magi didn't see Joseph because he 'happened not to be present at the time'. Maybe so. But, maybe also, St Matthew's statement means much more than we give it credit for. And alongside St Luke's account of the shepherds, it might be seen in a different light.

The shepherds saw 'Mary and Joseph. And the baby lying in the manger.' The bustle and strain of the birth is over. And there's a certain peace and order in the house. Could it be, by contrast, that St Matthew's note that the Magi saw 'the child with his mother Mary,' describes the scene not very long after the delivery of the child? And what the Magi are seeing is the new mother – like any other new mother – cherishing her just-born son, and nestling him to her bosom?

Did the Wise Men, in fact, arrive even before the Shepherds?

That's the end of the questions. Now to try to feel our way through St Matthew's account.

The Wise Men have arrived at what, they believe, is the right destination. They're seeking 'the new-born King of the Jews'. And, for them, the obvious and natural place to look for him is Jerusalem. It's the capital city, the place where kings reign, and kings are born.

And a beautiful city it is. A king's city. Oh, it had its squalid parts … but look at the beauty and grace and strength in some of its buildings. The Temple in honour of the Jews' God Jehovah, the huge marble blocks of its walls gleaming white in the early sun. And walk down to the far corner of this tight-packed, high-walled city, and see the powerful grandeur of the palaces which Herod the king had built and where he lives. The parklands around it, the wide, wide square where, it seemed, travellers from the world over dallied and gossiped, and seemed at home.

And yet, and yet, the people they met in the city scowled darkly, and seemed reluctant to talk when they told them of the mission they were on, and asked where they would find the new-born king.

The city knew nothing about a king, new-born or otherwise. In the taverns, where strong wine loosened tongues, they'd have been glad of a new king … any king … to replace the tyrant they had. But they talked softly, whispering, as though they told secrets, their eyes glancing, watching for faces they didn't trust. Falling silent when a stranger they didn't know stood too close and waited too long.

The king had spies everywhere, they confided. Everywhere. Listening. And reporting to the king. A man could die for speaking out of turn. There was a time, they said, when the king would disguise himself, and walk the city streets. And join the gossip and the chatter. Always listening, listening, for those who might criticise the king, and speak badly of him. And those who did paid dearly for their opinions.

He didn't do it nowadays, though. He couldn't. He was a sick man. Dying, the rumour was … but for them, not quickly enough.

But his informers trawled the streets, and the visitors could be sure that the king already knew of their presence in Jerusalem.

A priest near the Temple told the visitors they'd be better-off going back home. Jerusalem was troubled enough already with the king they had. There was too much intrigue in the city, he told them, too many plots against the king. And it wasn't just the ordinary people, who knew Herod only as a tyrant. It was the aristocracy of the city, the powerful ones. Members of the king's court, even. His brother, his brother's wife, his own son, would you believe …

The Magi couldn't believe.

Star or no star, the priest assured them, there was no new-born king. He couldn't be born in Jerusalem without Herod knowing. And, if he was born in Jerusalem,then he was dead already. Herod would make sure of that. Their search would only lead to trouble. For themselves. And also for Jerusalem, when Herod's network of spies had brought him the news. There'd be another bloodbath. Their best plan, the priest counselled them, would be to forget everything, and get away from the city quickly.

'Herod the king heard, and was troubled,' St Matthew writes.

Herod's story is a long story that takes a long time to tell. But, perhaps it will not seem out of place to tell some of it here. It might help to show how matters stood immediately prior to the appearance of the Magi in Jerusalem.

Herod heard because his spy-network was efficient. Their job, as Josephus describes it, was to 'fish out and inform'. And they did their job well.

And, of course, Herod was troubled.

After forty years of intrigue, plot and counter-plot, Herod's experience had taught him to be 'troubled' when rumours like this blew in the breeze. And the political astuteness by which he had become king and kept himself on the throne, would not permit him to treat this new rumour lightly.

But now, he had more cause then ever to be disturbed. The arrival of the Wise Men in Jerusalem came as a kind of climax to a bitter period for Herod.

He had, not long since, scotched a plot against his life by Alexander, one of his sons. The plot was revealed to the king by Trypho, his barber. Indeed, Trypho himself was being encouraged to do the deed. He, of all men, Tero, the encourager told him, could end the tyranny. He could cut the king's throat with the razor he was using to shave him. And there would be great rewards for Tero and the barber, because the instigator was none else than the king's own son, Alexander.

Herod was a sick man, a very sick man, after years of suffering and constant, wracking pain. He could do without people, not least his own flesh and blood, trying to kill him.

The king was grateful to the barber for his frank and open revelation. And dealt immediately with the situation. Tero, an old soldier, already in jail, and three hundred of his comrades in jail with him, were brought to trial, and convicted. Along with Trypho, the barber. And Tero's son. They were all stoned to death. All three-hundred-and-three of them. With, as Josephus explains, the multitude stoning them 'with whatsoever came to hand, and thereby slew them.'

The king dealt with Alexander, his son, as well. And another son, Aristobulus, who had given him enough bother. They both were taken secretly to Samaria, and strangled there.

But there was more.

Having solved the problem of Trypho, Tero, Alexander and Aristobulus, Herod now had to face the opposition of a group of Pharisees. These were powerful, influential men, held in great respect for their learning in the law, and considered by all to be highly favoured by God. They formed an Association of those who refused allegiance to the Emperor and the King himself.

Herod found it difficult to take them seriously. He was a Sadduccee, and disdained anybody who could believe in such a thing as the resurrection from the dead. But the Pharisees did.

There was nothing secret about the Pharisees' Association.

They made their objectives clear – to oppose, by all and any means, Roman power in Judaea, and to remove Herod from the Jewish throne. And all Jerusalem knew about them.

It was their openness, perhaps that saved them. Had they intrigued and plotted, Herod might have been concerned. But they didn't. So Herod couldn't take them seriously.

He didn't dismiss them. Herod dismissed nothing. But he bore them patiently for a while. Till his network informed him that there were some six thousand in Jerusalem who'd become members of the Pharisee Association.

Herod smarted at that. But he smarted even more when they informed him of the prophecy the Association had put out.

They claimed to be divinely inspired with the gift of foreknowledge of things to come. Their prophecy was that 'God hath resolved that the rule of Herod shall be ended, and that his decendants shall not inherit it.'

The king's spies could not have realised that they were rubbing salt into Herod's already hurting wound. Their sifting had found another prophecy put out by the Pharisee Association. About Jochebed, the wife of the king's own brother, Pheroras. Jochebed was expecting a child. That very child, soon to be born, the Association's prophecy proclaimed, was the Messiah.

 Herod reacted. Immediately. He arrested four of the leaders of the Association. He ordered them to recant, to swear allegiance, and declare both their prophecies a nonsense. They refused. And expected to be put to death for their obdurate stedfastness. Their punishment, however, was a crippling fine. To be paid within three days, the king ordered.

Herod's outwardly lenient approach was, in fact, like everything he did, a subtle manoeuvre.

If the Association of six-thousand couldn't raise the money to pay, it meant that they were people, despite all their bravado, of no real substance. And given time, could be easily dealt with. On the other hand, the fine paid would mean they had very rich friends, in very high places.

What hurt Herod, but didn't surprise him, was the realisation that a paid fine could only mean royal patronage ... somebody in his own household and court.

The Pharisee Association paid the fine. Within the stipulated three days.

Herod was grieved and sickened. Would he ever be free of this godforsaken family, this toadying household who hid their treachery under the cloak of docile servitude?

His sister, Salome, though he didn't trust her, and had forced her to marry a man she never wanted to marry, seemed to be the only one with any concern for the king. She also had her finger on the pulse of all that went on in the family and the king's court.

Salome suggested names. Herod repeated each name as he heard it from his sister. And pronounced the punishment. The prinicpal officers of the Pharisee Association were to be burned alive. It was Herod's twist of sadistic irony. He was spoiling the Pharisees' hope of a resurrection. Burning them would leave them no body to be resurrected. Nineteen other members of the Association would be beheaded.

The names of members of his household came next.

And sick, broken Herod, who spent every waking moment in agonising pain, cried as he listened. The two men on whom he depended, whom he trusted as friends. Bagoas! Carus!

Carus, who, Josephus says, 'exceeded all men of that time in comeliness,' was the king's catamite. He shared his bed. Now he was amongst those who conspired against him, and wished him dead.

Bagoas was his chamberlain. Poor Bagoas. A eunuch from his youth, he had been beguiled into membership of the Association with glowing promises of a future he never dreamed possible. When the new king, the Messiah had set up his new kingdom, Bagoas would marry. And the king would bestow on him the gift of fathering children. Bagoas would be beheaded. Carus would die in a man's embrace. He would be strangled.

Four other women who had played minor parts as conspirators were to be strangled along with Carus.

Now, it was the king's immediate family. They, too, were

amongst the conspirators. Not that any of them was motivated by any great conviction about the Association's principles. It was enough that the Association's aims to remove Herod from the throne coincided with theirs. They were content to use the Association as a means of gaining their own ends.

Doris. She had been Herod's first wife. Long since divorced, she still lived in the palace, had all the privileges of a queen, and managed the royal household. She had waited long enough for revenge. She also wanted the throne for Antipater, the son she had borne to Herod.

Her punishment? She might have expected to join the rest of those being executed. But she didn't. Instead, she was banished from the palace for ever, sent out as a pauper, deprived of all rights, titles, properties and pensions.

Jochebed. The wife of the king's brother, Pheroras. There was only a long and bitter hatred between Jochebed and the king. Herod considered her as no better than a slut, and reckoned his brother should never have married her. And would be well-advised to be rid of her. Jochebed it was who had paid the fine imposed on the four leaders of the Association. Her action not only rescued the four themselves, but saved the whole membership of the Association from financial ruin. The Association's prophecy was that she should be the mother of the Messiah. It didn't concern Jochebed that gossips said the Association acted as they did simply to reciprocate her generosity.

Herod saw her as a threat. And could not shake the Association's prophecy from his mind. And he could write a long list of Jochebed's offences. And some of them, at least, warranted the death penalty. She had protected those who plotted against the kingdom. The conspirators who had been tried and sentenced, she had enabled to escape. Over the years, she had studiously fomented a quarrel between his brother and himself, and brought them into a state of war. She had abused the king's virgin daughters, Roxana and Salome, his children by a former wife.

Her punishment? He might have killed her, as, indeed, he

might have executed Doris. But that wasn't easy, nor politic. The nation still remembered the execution of his two sons Alexander and Aristobulus. He would invite even deeper hatred were he to execute two women of the family.

Jochebed's punishment was, in fact, delayed for some time. And then, Pheroras, her husband, and herself were exiled from Jerusalem, and forced to live on the far side of the river Jordan, administering a small principality.

Herod dismissed his brother's membership of the Association. Pheroras was an honest fool. He could, and quite often did, disagree with the king. And made no bones about it. But he could never be disloyal. If Pheroras had joined up with the Pharisee association, it was only to please his wife, Jochebed, whom he loved blindly.

Salome had kept the bitter wine till the end. The king's son, Antipater.

But the king was in no mood to listen to Salome's complaints against Antipater. He was the son he was grooming to succeed him as king. He could see only good in Antipater. And would hear nothing that might say otherwise. But Herod would live to regret his so simple trust.

The day was to come – a few years later – when this very Antipater would plot to have his father poisoned. And with a carefully laid plan never to be implicated.

It happened, in fact, some years after the Wise Men's visit and, strictly speaking, is not part of our business at the moment. But maybe it's not entirely out of place to tell the story, as a kind of round-off to Herod's life-story. The man had his own troubles to put up with.

Antipater cajoled his uncle Pheroras to do the poisoning, with poison specially brought in from Alexandria. Antipater himself would already be in Rome while it was all happening, with two letters from his father for the Emperor Augustus.

One letter was a formal note, commending his son to the Emperor. The second contained a copy of the king's will, and a request that Caesar would graciously grant his wish to name his son, Antipater, as his successor.

The Emperor, it might be said, when he met the young man, was impressed by his filial devotion. So impressed, that he told him he was wrongly named. He should be called, not Anti-pater but Philo-pater, so deep was his love for his father. Little did the generous Emperor know!

The plot, however, failed. Pheroras had neither the stomach nor the heart to kill his own brother. Herod learnt about the plot … having tortured a few women servants into making a confession. Antipater was recalled from Rome, and imprisoned, after an emotional trial when he was convicted of parricide.

Time passed.

Herod is dying, and in such crucifying pain that he tries to kill himself with a fruit-knife. He is brought the news that Antipater has tried to bribe the jailer to break his chains and loose him from prison.

It was almost Herod's last act. He ordered that his son, Antipater be tortured till he was dead. And he named Archelaus as his successor. Five days later, the king himself was dead.

But that's jumping a bit far ahead. The Antipater episode is still in the future.

For the moment Herod has to deal with the Magi.

Their arrival in Jerusalem when they did, and on such a mission, cannot but have given Herod pause. He had dealt with his enemies, but the prophecy of the Pharisee Association still festered and fretted in his mind.

Herod, of course, could do something about it. The rest of Jerusalem, though, was powerless. Those who were opposed to the king waited for the repercussions they had grown to expect whenever Herod's felt his position threatened. The favoured ones suffered palpitations also. But for a different reason. They stood or fell according to Herod's ability to keep his balance. Their fortunes hung on a hinge whose centre-pin was Herod.

Herod the king was equal to the situation.

His move may have been motivated by the Wise Men's search scratching the scar left in his mind by the Pharisees. But, he would scotch the nonsense by having Israel's religious authority rule on the origins and birthplace of the Messiah. The move was certainly spurred by Herod's old habit of being one step ahead of his rivals. It had secured him in days gone by when threatened by Cleopatra of Egypt; it had preserved him with Caesar when the Jews complained against him; it had protected him against the plots by his own family and court. And, whether or not the present situation constituted any real threat, the king's old habit shaped the king's approach.

The visitors to his capital on their quest for the Messiah, have no notion as to where to find him. By the time Herod decides to meet them, he will have the advantage of them. He will know.

'And when he had brought together all the chief priests and scribes of the people, he asked them where the Messiah was to be born.'

Herod wanted an answer to a religious question. So he called the people who could be expected to know the answer. It suited his purpose to summon the Sanhedrin. But a somewhat depleted Sanhedrin ... depleted, indeed, by Herod himself.

As long as thirty years earlier, he had destroyed, not only the authority of the Sanhedrin, when it presumed to oppose him, but the Sanhedrin itself. On his accession, he had killed all its members except one. The man who remained was Babha ben Buta. But, on Herod's orders, Babha ben Buta's eyes were gouged out. Any little authority the council might now have, was of Herod's granting, and dependent on his whim.

The Council assembled, Herod asked his question. 'Where is the Messiah to be born?'

The learned men replied, quoting loosely, but giving the sense of the seven hundred year old prophecy of Micah. 'In Bethlehem of Judaea, for it is written thus through the prophet, "Thou, Bethlehem, in the land of Judah, art by no means least among the rulers of Judah, for out of thee a leader will come who shall rule my people Israel".'

The session, as St Matthew writes it, is brief. Whether or not the king's advisers offered any more information or comment, we have no way of knowing. But St Matthew's curt presentation gives a feeling of the contempt in which the priests and scribes of the people held Herod.

This ruler of the Jews had no idea of the nation's prophecies that rose effortlessly in the mind, and slid readily from the lips of any Jew worthy of the name!

The interview was ended. It was now time to examine the capital's visitors.

'Then Herod, having secretly called the Magi, tried to learn precisely from them when the star appeared, and sent them to Bethlehem, saying, "Go, and make exact enquiries about the child, and when you find him bring me word, that I too may come and worship him".'

The Magi were easily found. They had been under surveillance from the time they began their enquiries about their new-born king. Herod's spy network throughout his kingdom was employed to 'fish out and inform him' of this kind of activity. And their arrival, in any case, could hardly go unnoticed. It wasn't just a handful of men. It was the Magi themselves, plus their guards and their servants. And all on camels!

They were secretly brought. And they met a Herod who was so well informed that they suffered something of an inquisition as he searched and probed about the star whose appearance had started them on their quest. And he gave them the vital piece of information they needed. 'He sent them to Bethlehem.' But with a king's command. 'Go and make exact enquiries about the child. And when you find him, bring me word, that I too may come and worship him.'

What exactly Herod had in mind when he issued his command, can only be guessed at. Judge what Herod is saying now, by what he did later, and it would be natural to assume that he already had murder in mind.

But, if his later act was the rash act of a despot who had waited long beyond the limits of patience for the Magi to return, is it not possible to believe that Herod genuinely meant what he said?

Look at it this way. If murder were Herod's intention, then depending on the Magi was a singularly naïve way of setting

about it. He had better means at his disposal. He had so many al-
ternatives. He had ample experience. His spies, given no more
time than the Magi might take, could have led them to the door
of the house. Using total strangers might have a subtlety, a novelty that would appeal to a despot. But for Herod's serious business, if he had murder in mind, it seems too haphazard. It's not
up to Herod's usual standard.

St Matthew writes the record coldly. He makes no comment,
adverse or otherwise, on Herod. He offers no assessment of his
character, passes no judgement. In such a non-committal atmosphere, it would be hasty, to say the least, to write down the
Herod who meets the Magi as a diplomatic deceiver already
plotting infanticide.

But, is there anything about Herod himself that might hint
that, for once in his blood-spattered career, the man meant what
he was saying?

Doesn't it say something that after the Pharisee conspiracy,
the two who were left alive were Jochebed and the infant son she
claimed was the Messiah? Herod could be a tyrant. But he was
also a man. And his history displays his humanity and his heart
for the people he governed. It tells of his temper. But nowhere
does it establish that his mind and brain automatically and immediately bent to murder as soon as he scented opposition.

Being a half-Jew, it's not totally inconceiveable that he occa-
sionally felt Jewish emotions. He was opposed to the narrow na-
tionalism of the fanatics of the nation. But that does not mean he
was bereft of Jewish political sentiments and ambitions.

He dedicated himself to preserving the nation. And succeeded.
And the long history of Israel suggests that his means of achiev-
ing his objective, while they may have been no better, they certainly were no worse than those of Israel's most famous kings.
And he, like them, considered he was an instrument in God's
hands for the welfare of the nation.

He rebuilt the Temple as a thankoffering to God. Before the
building work started, Herod made a speech to the people, explaining why.

Josephus records it in his *Antiquities of the Jews*. It's a long speech, but there are parts that are important. They give an insight into the man.

'With God's assistance,' Josephus reports him as saying, 'I have advanced the nation of the Jews to a degree of happiness which they never had before ... I am now, by God's will, your governor, and I have had peace a long time ... and, what is the principal thing of all, I am at amity with, and well regarded by the Romans who, if I may say so, are the rulers of the whole world. I will do my endeavour to correct that imperfection which hath arisen from the necessity of our affairs, and the slavery we have been under formerly. And make a thankful return, after the most pious manner to God, for what blessings I have received from him, by giving me this kingdom, and that by rendering his Temple as complete as I am able.'

The same man might also, in his own way, and for his own reasons, have been wishing for the Messiah. Indeed, if the report by St Matthew represents in any precise way the question which Herod put to his advisers, then it reflects something of Herod's political, if not his religious longing. The Magi had come seeking a mere king in Judah. Herod's question was about the Messiah.

And his wish to worship the new-born king is not so absurd, if Herod considered him the Messiah, and saw in him the great deliverer of Israel.

Herod, by now, was a man of sixty-seven. A desperately sick man, worn, broken, and made even older by a reign that had begun forty years earlier. If he could claim, in the eighteenth year of his reign, that he had good relations with the Romans, it wasn't because he loved them, but because the friendship was vital for the life and well-being of Israel. If the truth were known, he hated the Romans, and all things Roman. His political ambition was to see the Jewish nation independent. Its ultimate achievement, though, would mean driving out the Roman oppressor. And this was a task Herod didn't consider himself equipped to undertake. But the promised Messiah, it was fervently believed, would do just this.

Is it impossible, then, that Herod, sick, worn and old, knowing that his reign could not last much longer, could have been moved by the prospect? He had preserved the nation for this day. He could have no better successor than Messiah himself.

'Bring me word, that I too may come and worship him,' may reveal more of Herod's heart than even he would be prepared to admit, or his people prepared to accept.

Honest man or consummate liar, the audience was ended.

It was night when the Magi left the palace. They searched the speckled darkness of the sky, and found again the star by which they had plotted their course from the East to Jerusalem. 'When they saw the star, they rejoiced very greatly.' And by it they plotted the last stage of their months-long journey, the road to Bethlehem, realising that the directions Judah's reigning king had given them coincided prescisely with their own navigational calculations. They followed their journey by the star, till they came to the house.

'And when they had entered the house, they saw the child with his mother Mary. They fell down, and worshipped him.'

They had set out expecting to greet a new-born king. They had come, therefore, with the rich gifts they considered proper to present to a king, borne carefully the journey through in treasure chests. 'And opening their caskets, they offered to him gifts, gold and frankincense and myrrh.

'Being instructed in a dream not to go back to Herod, they withdrew to their own country by another road.'

St Matthew barely opens the door on the Holy Family. Like St Luke, he seems at pains to protect their privacy. Conscious of his responsibilty, he establishes the occasion, yet affords his readers no more than a glimpse, hasting them away, to be concerned with other matters.

He now turns to look at the doubts that shaped in the minds of the Magi, and made them change their plans about returning to Herod.

From St Matthew's record, it looks clear that the Magi had no cause to suspect Herod's motives during their audience with him. He had, after all, given them the answer to their question, 'Where is he who is born King of the Jews?' And they had got to Bethlehem on his advice.

What made them change their mind? What shaped their dream?

Did they, during their visit ot the house, or as they prepared in Bethlehem for their return journey to Jerusalem, gather gossip and information about Herod that forced them to see the king in a new and sinister light? Did they, on reflection, imagine tones of treachery in what once sounded like an honest man's desire, 'Bring me word, that I, too, may come and worship him'?

The record implies that the Wise Men's contravention of Herod's command was entirely their own decision, as the result of a dream. That they dreamt doesn't make them unique. That their dream was shaped by news and gossip picked up in Bethlehem, would not be unusual. And men who had arrived in Jerusalem on the basis of their interpretation of the stars in their courses, could as readily re-route their journey home as the result of a dream.

And that, whatever the cause of the dream, they did.

Whether or not it was the best decision the Magi could have made, we can never know. Though it's tempting to wonder what might have happened had they, instead, gone back to Herod.

Would Herod have come and worshipped? And would the history of the nation, in consequence, have been differently written? Would Herod have ordered the death of the infants in Bethlehem? Or would he, instead, have been impressed by the Magi's information, and been content to conclude that the little family in the little town were so obviously without political influence or ambition?

But they didn't go back. Instead they returned to their own country by another route. And their change of mind sparked-off a chain of reactions which they, safely out of harm's way, may not even have heard about.

CHAPTER ELEVEN

Rites and Ceremonies
St Luke 2:21-39

When eight days were completed for circumcising him,
his name was called Jesus,
as he was called by the angel
before he was conceived in the womb.

When the days for their purification
according to the Law of Moses were completed,
they brought him up to Jerusalem to present him to the Lord,
(as it is written in the Law of the Lord,
'Everything male that opens the womb
shall be called holy to the Lord,')
and to offer a sacrifice
according to what is stated in the Law of the Lord,
a pair of doves, or two young pigeons.

The shepherds and the Magi have come and gone.

The house seemed empty after all the hustle and bustle of strangers arriving, and neighbours fussing, and thinking he was a lovely baby.

There's time, now, to get used to a baby in the house, and make arrangements with the Rabbi and the Mohel for the circumcision. And time, precious time, for Mary and Joseph to go on wondering why, and what did it all mean, and where would it all end.

'When eight days were completed for circumcising him, his name was called Jesus, as he was called by the angel before he was conceived in the womb.'

Jesus was no different from any other Jewish boy. And Jewish Mary and Joseph automatically and naturally followed the rule of their ancient religion which required the new-born son to be circumcised. It was fulfilling God's command to Abraham, and was the sign of God's Covenant with his people (Gen 17:5, 15).

And the rite had to be performed on the eighth day after the boy's birth. There was no departing from that time. It was the day Abraham and his sons were circumcised as a sign of God's Covenant. And so strict was the rule that even if the eighth day were a Sabbath, the boy was still circumcised (see Jn 7:22, 23). It is the boy's formal admission into the household of Israel.

It was a happy, sedate, friendly occasion, judging from St Lukes' presenation. The friends and neighbours in Bethlehem are gathered in the house. And there's a sense of pleasure in the place. They take delight in Joseph having brought his wife to his own native town for his son to be born there. It's good, they reckon, mumbling their approval one to the other. It's good that a descendant of David the Ephratite should be so proud of his descent that he would honour his son with being born in David's city.

Everything is set and ready. Including the empty seat – the chair of Elijah, the unseen participant in every ceremony of cir-cumcision. The prayers are said. The Sandak takes the child in his lap. The Mohel stoops, and performs the act of circumcision. And the ceremony is ended.

Now the boy will be named.

This time, there are no bossy, knowing relatives, as there were at John's circumcision a few months earlier. There is no argument about the name. It's a good name, they all agree. An honourable name, an historic name. And as they settle into eat-ing and drinking, they call to mind the great men of Israel, the saviours of the nation who bore the same name.

'His name was called Jesus,' St Luke reports. As, indeed, does St Matthew. But St Matthew makes it clear that Joseph it was who announced the name during the ceremony. 'He named him Jesus' (Mt 1:25).

St Luke is obviosly well aware of the fact, though he doesn't mention it. Instead, he gives a kind of flashback, to remind his readers of the angel Gabriel's appearance to Mary nine months earlier. It was then that Mary was instructed what name her child should be given.

St Luke reports, 'His name was called Jesus, as he was called by the angel before he was conceived in the womb.'

The name itself is the Greek form of the Hebrew name *Joshua*, which means *God is Salvation*. It was a common enough name in Israel. And, while famous men in Israel's past had adorned it with greatness, there was no particular reason why its meaning, when applied to this first-born son in a house in Bethlehem, should impress itself on the people at the ceremony.

St Luke seems to be at no pains to explain or draw-out the meaning of the name. Not yet. He is content to wait till it can be done in a suitable setting. And the setting is already in his mind – the Temple. The occasion is Mary's Purification rites, and the Presentation of her son.

St Luke writes, 'When the days of their purification according to the Law of Moses were completed, they brought him to Jerusalem to present him to the Lord, (as it is written in the Law of Moses, 'Everything male that opens the womb shall be called holy to the Lord,') and to offer a sacrifice according to what is stated in the Law, a pair of doves, or two young pigeons.'

Childbirth, the Hebrews considered, made the mother ceremonially 'unclean'. She could not, in consequence, touch anything that was considered sacred, because it was consecrated to God. She must wait a time till she was considered 'purified'. And during that waiting time, the woman stayed in her own house. She certainly would not go into the Temple, for fear that her 'uncleannes' would defile the sanctity of the Holy Place.

Giving birth to a boy meant waiting forty days. It was twice as long for a girl. Mary's days of 'purification,' then, lasted for forty days.

St Luke writes 'their' rather than 'her' purification, which seems strange. Usually, it is assumed that only the mother is made ceremonially 'unclean,' but not her child as well. But St

Luke, when he writes what he writes, obviously knows what he's doing. It could be, of course, that St Luke considers that the child, in so close contact with his mother, is deemed to be ceremonially unclean.

In any case, Mary could not enter the Temple until the end of the forty days. Then she could attend in the Temple, to present a thankoffering to God for her preservation throughout the pain and peril of childbirth. And, as the Law required, receive the rite of Purification (see Lev 12).

Came the day, the day to fulfil their obligation in the Temple.

It was about six miles from Bethlehem to Jerusalem. They could take their time, and still be there in about two hours.

They made an early start. Before the sun was properly risen. It was easier to travel in the cool. But the early start also meant they would not meet so many people on the road. And Mary would not come into contact with people who might defile her, and, in consequence, delay her attending in the Temple.

She travelled on a donkey. Not that Joseph would have it any other way. But today, more than ever, it was improtant. Walking the rough road, she might have risked walking somewhere or on something that would cause defilement that would put a stop to her going into the Temple. The donkey kept her off the ground. And that avoided the risks. Some women, after their forty days, rode on an ox to be sure they would not touch the ground.

Mary was making her way to Jersualem, cuddling her son, chatting with Joseph as they travelled along.

She knew the road well. In the past few months, she'd been along it three times already. It was dfferent, now, though. She felt easier in her mind, the old frets were going, and she was beginning to feel ordinary again. A proud young woman, nursing her new-born son.

Joseph walked alongside her, stepping the road, his staff making regular thumps, keeping time with his pace. Mary watched him. Poor Joseph. He had been through so much … but he seemed easier now, too. The stoop of worry had gone from his shoulders, and there was a new liveliness in his step.

He looked round to see that she was alright. Mary cuddled her son, and snuggled her shoulders, smiling back her assurance that she was grand. And she saw the smile crinkle over his beard. And the loving look in his eyes that spoke, telling her that the worst was over, and everything would be better now.

They could see the walls of Jerusalem now. They'd left the hills behind them. And they'd be in the city in no time.

'I was glad when they said unto me, let us go into the house of the Lord,' Joseph mumbled, as though he were talking to himself. But Mary heard it. And said, 'Amen.'

She nudged the donkey faster to keep up with Joseph's quickened walk. It seemed as though the beast realised it was near journey's end, and readily responded.

And then they were through the city gate. They were in Jerusalem!

A paddock-keeper near the gate agreed to take care of the donkey, and water and feed him while they were visiting the Temple.

And then they stood, taking in the spacious grandeur of the city's south-west corner, with houses that neither Bethlehem nor even Nazareth had ever seen. The High Priest's house over on their left. And then the broad square, with the palaces King Herod had built for himself, on one side. The wide, wide promenade, where they passed the Hall of the King's Council on their left-hand side. Beyond them, the bridge that spanned the valley between the two hills on which the city was built. The bridge would take them to the north-eastern corner of the city, where the Temple reared proud, beautiful, gleaming white, strong, as though it would last a thousand years.

Already, there were people streaming across the bridge. Travellers, pilgrims, priests, levites, Jerusalemites, men and women who were daily worshippers in the Temple.

Joseph kept close to Mary and her son, lest she should be jostled in the crowd.

On one side they could see deep down where the valley ran. And on the other side, spread out all round, the warren of con-

gested streets, their shops, cramped houses with children play-
ing on the parapetted roofs, and craftsmen's workshops, the
bazaars and market-stalls, waiting for the crowds that would
very soon be milling around them.

Joseph and Mary, with her child, made no delay in getting
across the bridge. And were glad to be in the space of the Court
of the Temple.

Not that it was any less busy here. Business and bargaining,
and buying and selling didn't stop at the boundary wall of the
Holy Temple.

The cattle-dealers were here, loudly touting the calves they
had for sale. And men selling lambs. And merchants with their
tight-packed cages of pigeons and doves for sale.

Worshippers would need one thing or the other as sacrificial
offerings. Beasts and birds, the dealers explained, had already
been examined and declared by the priest to be ceremonially
clean. The worshipper had to agree that it was a great convenience.
But for that conveninece, the pilgrim, the worshipper paid dearly.
And many more times the price that even the most crooked trader
in the marketplace beyond these holy walls would charge.

Before the day had even properly begun, they were moving
in with their stock, taking their places, setting up their stalls in
the porticoes around the Temple.

And, of course, the money-changers. They were already en-
sconcing themselves at their tables. They made their money easily,
and used the Ten Commandments of the Law of Moses to justify
their extortion.

Every Hebrew, no matter where he came from in the world,
was expected to pay his Temple taxes in Jerusalem. There were
twelve great trumpet-like containers inside the Temple to receive them.

No dues could be paid, no fees paid in the ordinary everyday
coinage, for it was almost certainly engraved with the Emperor's
head. And, because nobody dare bring a graven image into the
Holy Temple, the coinage must be exchanged for the Sanctuary
Shekel, *shekel hakodesh*, the shekel of the sanctuary.

Money-changers did the exchanging. And the worshippers paid expensively for the service – the going-rate of exchange plus at least five-per-cent commission.

It was hard to believe that the Sanhedrin and the High Priest of Israel could countenance such goings-on that robbed this holy place of every shred of sanctity.

Joseph bought two doves. Mary would need them as her thankoffering at the rite of Purification.

It's fashionable – not to say suitably sentimental – to assume that Mary's offering reveals the poverty of the Holy Family. But does it?

St Luke writes that Mary was 'to offer a sacrifice according to what is stated in the Law of the Lord, a pair of doves or two young pigeons.'

Granted that this is what the Book of Leviticus allows as the 'poor woman's ' offering (Lev 12: 8). But it may be that there's more to be said that might suggest caution before making a decision about the family's poverty. Doves, at this time, were not exactly the cheapest things available. The greed and avarice of Annas, the High Priest, and his family saw to that.

Annas was deeply involved in business and trading. He had a vested interest in the facilities afforded the traders and merchants and money-changers in the Temple precincts. And, indeed, sometimes spread into the Temple itself, taking space in the Court of the Gentiles. The shops and stalls and trading pitches were infamously known as 'The Booths of the sons of Annas.' (Jesus himself, in years to come, was to call them 'a den of thieves'.) The Talmud pours scorn and condemnation on the whole House of Annas – 'Woe to the House of Annas. Woe to their serpent's hiss ... They are High Priests; their sons are Keepers of the Treasury; their sons-in-law the Guardians of the people; and their servants beat the people with staves.'

Annas supplied olive-oil and doves to the Temple from his estate on the Mount of Olives. He had something of a monopoly in the olive-oil trade. He may not have quite cornered the market with the doves he bred on the same estate, but he still managed to make a rich profit.

Besides this sizeable stake, the priests increased the demand. They had multiplied the occasions in which doves were used for sacrifice. Increased demand increased the price. A dove sold for a golden denarius.

Before leaving the matter of Mary's 'poor woman' status, it may not appear too cheeky to make a suggestion.

Gold, it's worth recalling, was amongst the gifts the Magi presented on their arrival. Whatever the family's financial state was before the visit, after the visit, if they were not the richest family, they were certainly amongst the richest families in the little town of Bethlehem. And well-off enough to move Mary out of the 'poor woman' bracket.

Mary's father, Joachim, was reputedly a very rich and very generous man. It's said he gave away two thirds of his income – a third to the Temple, a third to the poor, and lived well on the rest. Whether he believed Mary's explanation of her pregnancy or not, it's hard to imagine so rich and generous a man leaving his daughter to live at subsistence level. And be classed as a 'poor woman' when it came to making her offering in the Temple.

And so the caution.

When all is said and done, it may well be that St Luke is not describing their poverty, but simply stating no more and no less than the rules and conditions prevailing in the Temple at the time.

At any rate, being able to afford two doves at a golden denarius apiece is hardly the badge of desolating poverty. Especially when it is remembered that Joseph has still to pay more money before he leaves the Temple with Mary and her son. He has still to buy five Sanctuary Shekels, the fee he will pay to the priest as the redemption price during Jesus's Presentation. And, like everybody else, he pays the going rate of exchange plus at least five per cent commission. The fee he pays is part of the priest's perquisites.

He bought the shekels. And, with a firm grip on the doves, himself and Mary joined the multitude of worshippers to watch the Dawn Ceremony.

Every face was turned, looking at the top of the Pinnacle of the Temple – the great rock that ran sheer down to the Kedron Valley, and formed the south-eastern corner of the boundary wall of the Temple precincts.

High upon the Pinnacle, the lone priest stood, searching across the valley to spy the sun sheening the crown of Olivet.

'The sun is shining,' he called. And waited till the cry came back from his companions far below him in the court.

'Is the sky lit up to Hebron?'

The priest looked out again, lingering on the sight of Olivet, freckled with pilgrim tents, moving sleepily to life with the early risers up to greet the new day. Then he looked to the far-off reaches of the land, spread north and west, his arms flung wide as though he would embrace it all.

'It is lit up,' he cried, 'And lit as far as Hebron.' Taking a last look, he descended the rock to join his brother priests and return with them to wait in Temple silence till the day's first sacrifice and the silver trumpets sounded throughout Jerusalem.

The Dawn Ceremony was over.

The priests gone, the watchers moved. Women, their children in their arms, who had come to the Temple for their Purification after childbirth, made their way, chattering, to the Court of the Women.

Mary and Joseph went with them. But once at the entrance to the Court of the Women, Joseph left her, to wait for her under the porticoes that ran along the east wall.

It was an awesome place. Mary was overwhelmed by it all, hardly seeing what she looked at, aware only of the splendour rising in steps to the crowning glory of the Sanctuary, its towering, gilded walls dazzling back the brightness of the morning sun.

No sound now, but the mumble as women offered thanksgiving for their safe delivery, and prayed for the children, hoping their prayers would rise with the morning's incense, and be heard by God.

Nine blasts on the silver trumpets pierced the silence, giving warning that the sacrifice of the morning had been offered, and signalling the time for morning prayer.

And then the great Nicanor Gate was opened. Looking beyond the crescent steps supporting it, Mary could see the Great Altar, and the golden doors of the Holy Place, topped by its golden vine from which hung grapes in clusters taller than a man.

A Levite accepted the two doves she presented as her Purification offering. He brought the offering to the Court of the Priests where it was burned on the altar of the morning sacrifice.

A priest returned, and with the blood of her sacrifice, he sprinkled Mary, pronouncing her ritually clean. Her forty days were ended. Now she could return to worshipping in the congregation.

Her task now was, with her husband, to redeem her son.

The law of Moses required that a firstborn son be presented to God, and consecrated to God's service, like Samuel in the ancient days. The law, however, allowed that parents, if they wished, might be absolved from this obligation, and 'redeem' their sons, by paying five sanctuary shekels instead (see Num 18:15).

Joseph joined Mary by the steps, and took the infant in his arms.

A priest came, and stood before them.

'My wife, who is an Israelite,' began Joseph, 'has borne as her firstborn, a male child which I now give to you, as God's representative.'

'Which would you rather do?' enquired the priest, 'Give up your firstborn, who is the first son of his mother, to Jehovah, or redeem him for five shekels, after the shekel of the Sanctuary?'

'This is my firstborn,' Joseph replied. 'Here, take unto thee the five shekels due for his redemption.' He stretched out his hand, still speaking as he offered the redemption price, 'Blessed art thou, O Lord our God, King of the universe, who hast sanctified us with thy commandments, and commanded us to perform the redemption of a son. Blessed art thou, O Lord our God,

King of the universe, who hast maintained us, and preserved us to enjoy this season.'

The priest took the money in his right hand, and passed it round the infant's head. Then laid his left hand on his brow. 'This money is instead of this child. May this child be brought to life, to the law, and to the fear of heaven. And as he has been brought to be ransomed, so may he enter into the law, and good deeds.'

The ceremony was near its end. Joseph and Mary bowed their heads as the priest laid both his hands upon their infant's head, and pronounced his benediction: 'God make thee as Ephraim and Manasseh. The Lord bless and preserve thee. The Lord lift up his countenance upon thee, and give thee peace. Length of days be gathered unto thee. And God keep thee from all evil, and save thy soul.'

Their son's redemption was complete.

Mary and Joseph turned to leave, making their way through those who still waited to redeem their firstborn sons.

'There was a man in Jerusalem whose name was Simeon. This man was righteous and devout, expecting the consolation of Israel; and the Holy Spirit was upon him. It had been revealed to him by the Holy Spirit that he would not see death before he saw the Lord's Messiah. Led by the Spirit he came into the Temple; and when the parents had brought in the child Jesus to do concerning him according to the custom of the law, he received him into his arms, praised God and said, "Master, now thou art releasing thy servant in peace according to thy saying; for my eyes have seen thy deliverance which thou hast prepared before all the peoples, light to be a revelation to the Gentiles, and glory for thy people Israel".'

His father and his mother were astonished at what was being said about him. Simeon blessed them and said to Mary, his mother, "This child is appointed to cause the fall and rise of many is Israel, and to be a sign which is spoken against (a sword will pierce your own soul), that the thoughts of many minds may be revealed."

There was a prophetess Anna, daughter of Phanuel, of the tribe

*of Asher. She was far advanced in years; she had lived with a hus-
band seven years from her virginity, and she was a widow of eighty-
four years. She did not leave the Temple, serving God night and day
with fasts and prayers. She came near at that time and made acknowledgement to God, and spoke about him to all who were
expecting redemption in Jerusalem.'*

St Luke outlines the whys and wherefores of Mary and Joseph's
visit to Jerusalem. And gives the impression that he is about to
tell of all that went on in the Temple.

But he doesn't. Unexpectedly, he changes course, and leaves
his readers to recollect for themselves what happens in the age-
old rites of Purification and Presentation. Instead, he jars his
reader's mind, turning abruptly to the moment, the event, the
drama that has been in his mind since he first reported, 'His
name was called Jesus.'

Now, he will explain and enlarge on the meaning of the name
given to Mary's son at his circumcison. And in his own way.

What St Luke does is important. But the way he does it has its
own fascination. He draws his reader into a scene where he can
see what's happening, and hear what's being said. It's theatre at
its best. It might have been written for television.

He has done it before.

He didn't just tell us about the birth. He drew us sensitively
into the intimacy of the house in Bethlehem, inviting us almost
to be present at the very moment the Word became flesh. 'She
brought forth her firstborn son. And bedded him in the manger.'
He encouraged us to stand with the shepherds in the field. We
heard the angel's message, and the praise the angelic host raised
to heaven. We felt the shepherds' exhilaration, and heard them
as they decided to go to Bethlehem. And heard them again as
they talked excitedly in the house ... and their noisy departure
through the streets of the quiet little town.

Now he's doing it again. And he manages the scene like an
artist.

Nobody leaves the stage, yet the player delivering the lines is
the only person on whom we are drawn to concentrate.

Look at the scene.

The crowd in the Court of the Women is blanked out. We lose sight of the little family who, up to a fraction ago, we watched so concentratedly.

Dramatically, the whole stage is blacked, and a glaring spotlight carves a space in the darkness, as the evangelist switches attention to the character suddenly entering.

'Behold! There was a man in Jerusalem whose name was Simeon.'

An old man. The beard tidily trimmed. The robes round the body that the years have shrunk, making the robes too loose, too large for the frame that carries them.

The spotlight holds him, establishing him. 'This man was righteous and devout, expecting the consolation of Israel.'

The light no longer glares, and the focus tightens, examining him, slowly, slowly, his attitudes, his longings, his premonitions. 'And the Holy Spirit was upon him. And it had been revealed to him that he would not see death before he saw the Lord's Messiah.'

The eyes of all who watch move with him as he moves to take the central position. 'And he came in the Spirit into the Temple.' In the spotlight's edge, the eye makes out the family once lost to sight. 'And when the parents had brought in the child Jesus to do for him according to the custom of the law ...'

The spotlight stops, The moving Simeon halts, now centre stage, face to face with the parents and their child.

Searching, probing, the light's beam exaggerates the sheen of white from the swaddled form in Mary's arms, registering the child as the object of Simeon's rivetted attention and almost ecstatic thoughts. The premonition that he would not die till he had seen the Lord's Messiah must surely now be being fulfilled.

This devout and righteous man has come into the Temple, prompted by the Holy Spirit to expect some great thing. And the first thing his eyes light on is this child whose name is *Jesus, Joshua* , and means *Salvation, Deliverance.*

How closely St Luke brings us to the heart of things. He has already brought us as glimpsing witnesses to the birth. But stand now where Simeon stands. We're even closer now. And for longer.

'Then he took him up into his arms.' How close is that!

'He praised God,' writes St Luke. He doesn't report the words of praise. But he reports the words, the murmur-soft, whispered words old Simeon speaks as he gazes on the face and form of the child he cradles tenderly in his arms.

'Lord, now thou art releasing thy servant in peace, according to thy saying,' the man speaks, moved with wonder and emotion. 'For my eyes have seen *thy salvation* …'

And St Luke is careful to record the words, for this is the nub of the meaning of the name he would explain – *Jesus*, the Greek form of the Hebrew *Joshua* – the name announced by angels to Mary and Joseph as the name by which Mary's son will be called. The name that he was given at the time of his circumcision.

Simeon's expression in Hebrew which we translate 'Thy salvation,' is *Joshuatika*. 'My eyes have seen *thy Jesus, thy Joshua, thy Salvation*.' Simeon goes on to say that this *Joshuatika* is '*thy salvation* which thou hast prepared before all the peoples, light to be a revelation to the Gentiles, and glory for thy people Israel.'

Simeon and the words he speaks are vital to St Luke's explanation and enlargement of the meaning of the name 'Jesus'. They tell not only who Jesus is, they tell also what he has been born to be and to accomplish. Simeon, as St Luke presents him, knows that in holding this child in his arms, he is looking at the personification of God's salvation; holding in his arms the Word made flesh. Nursing the swaddled Saviour of Mankind – Jew and Gentile alike.

How close is that!

Mary and Joseph can only stand awe-stricken at what Simeon is saying. As St Luke puts it, 'His father and mother were astonished at what was being said about him.' They both would dearly love to know what it all meant.

But, as though the aged Simeon knew what was in their minds, he leans towards them.

Simeon blessed them. And then spoke to Mary. 'Your child,' he tells her, 'is set for the fall of many in Israel, for many will reject him. But also for the rising of many who will believe on him, and live. He is sent as a sign which shall be spoken against, and will meet reproach and contradiction, which will reveal the thoughts of many hearts ...'

Future events already casting long shadows.

But Mary did not understand. Nor did her husband, Joseph.

Only the old man still spoke. 'Indeed, a sword shall pierce thine own soul also ...'

St Luke might have stopped there, leaving the mind searching after the tragedy and sorrow foreshadowed in the old man's words. But he does not end there. His stage is still full of people lost to our vision in the darkness that shapes the spotlight brightness where Mary and Joseph and Simeon and the child stand revealed.

The spotlight loses its shafting glare as the stage eases into light again, giving colour again, and movement to the company that throngs in the Court of the Women, where women, after the rite of Purification, wait with their husbands to pay for the redemption of their firstborn sons.

Enter Anna. An old lady, 'advanced in years,' as St Luke describes her. She had been married for seven years. She is now 'a widow of eighty-four years.'

This must mean she was eighty-four years of age. It can hardly mean the years of her widowhood. If it does, she was a lady of the most advanced years. Married at fourteen, say. Her husband died when she was twenty-one, were she eighty-four years a widow, then, at the time she arrived on the scene with Mary and Joseph, she was 14 plus 7 plus 84. That equals 105. That's 'far advanced in years' with a vengeance. It seems likely, in the circumstances that St Luke is saying she was eighty-four years old.

She was a prophetess who lived in a room in the Temple. 'She did not leave the Temple, serving God night and day with fasts and prayers.'

An elderly, devout lady.

Simeon had hardly stopped speaking when Anna arrived.

She came 'in that instant,' writes St Luke and, like Simeon had done, 'made acknowledgement to God,' offering him thanks.

She obviously heard something of what Simeon had been saying, and looked at the infant in his arms. And began to echo his speech to the mothers and fathers waiting in the Temple in Jerusalem for their sons' redemption.

When he reports what Anna spoke about, St Luke has a subtle play on words for the reader who wants to notice it. He writes, she 'spoke about him to all who were expecting redemption in Jerusalem.'

Did she just speak about him? Is that all she did?

St Luke's play of the word 'redemption' wants to imply that she did much more than that. To those who came to Jerusalem for the rite of redemption, Anna spoke of Jesus, the sign and token of God's redemption, already available. Freely.

As Anna ends her speech, St Luke draws attention away from the overall scene, focusing now on the couple with whom he began. He writes, *When they had performed all the requirements of the law of the Lord, they returned to Galilee, to their city Nazareth ...'*

St Luke has, to all intents and purposes, ended his account of the birth of Jesus. He has written all that he thinks necessary. All that he knows, perhaps.

But, in giving the impression that the Holy Family went to Nazareth immediately after their visit to the Temple, he is short-circuiting history.

There is a deal more to happen and a deal more time is to pass between the Temple and their eventual return to Nazareth. There is still the Flight into Egypt, the slaughter of the infants, Herod's death, Joseph's dream before the family returns to Nazareth.

But we have to depend on St Matthew for all that, because St Luke makes no mention of it.

Why not? For all the attempts that have been made, there is still no definitive answer. Maybe, though, St Luke's leaving them out is not too remarkable,

St Matthew, for reasons best known to himself, writes noth-

ing about matters like Mary and Joseph living in Nazareth before the nativity; Mary's stay with her cousin Elizabeth; the circumstances that brought them to Bethlehem; the Presentation in
the Temple.

Whether or not St Luke knew about the Magi, the Flight into
Egypt, the slaughter of the innocents, is a bit beside the point. He
doesn't include them.

St Luke is a polished writer. A man who knows his craft, and
so obviously enjoys it. He knows what he's doing. Reading his
whole record, the feeling is that, all the time, consciously or un-
consciously, he is building to the crowning glory of the story of
the birth of Jesus.

With Simeon's declaration and prophecy, and Anna's preach-
ing to those who looked for redemption, St Luke brings his audience to the story's climax.

His closing paragraph serves simply to close the act. Maybe
he does short-circuit history, but the climax shines, gold, majestic, crystal-clear. *Joshuatika ra'u 'enai* ... My eyes have seen thy
salvation.

CHAPTER TWELVE

Flight
St Matthew 2:13-15

When they had withdrawn,
the angel of the Lord appeared to Joseph in dream, saying,
'Get up, take the child and his mother,
and flee to Egypt, and stay there till I tell you,
for Herod is going to seek the child to destroy him.'

He got up, took the child and his mother in the night,
and withdrew to Egypt,
and was there till the death of Herod;
that what was spoken by the Lord
through the prophet might be fulfilled,
when he said, Out of Egypt I called my son.

Here is divine intervention with a vengeance. And St Matthew meticulously registers it.

The instruction by the angel to Joseph in his dream, as St Matthew presents it, is fascinating for its detail.

The direction by the angel to Joseph is not simply to take his wife and child, and go. Their destination is designated, and the duration of their stay explained as a matter about which he must wait for further instruction at the appropriate time. Even the reason for his having to escape from Bethlehem is explained to him … a piece of advice which suggests that, at the time of this visitation, Joseph had no cause or reason to fear any attacks or threats from any quarter, least of all from King Herod in Jerusalem.

But the heavenly messenger leaves Joseph in no doubt. 'Herod is going to seek the child to destroy him.'

St Matthew in his accounts, doesn't make it clear how long it was after the Magi 'had withdrawn' that the 'angel of the Lord appeared to Joseph.' It's unlikely that it was as soon as they had left the house. Was it when they had departed from Bethlehem? Or from the province of Judah? From Palestine itself?

What is clear, though, abundantly clear from St Matthew's record of the angelic mesage is that the direction to leave was given to Joseph well in advance of Herod's decision to institute the slaughter in Bethlehem.

Joseph wasted no time in complying with the command. Indeed, the impression St Matthew gives is that Joseph dreamed the dream, wakened, was up, packed, got his wife and child out of bed in the middle of the night, and was on the way. 'The angel of the Lord appeared to Joseph in a dream, saying, "Get up, take the child and his mother, and flee to Egypt." ... He got up, took the child and his mother in the night, and withdrew to Egypt ...'

There are no details of the route they took, nor of the place in which they lived when they got to Egypt.

Tradition has it that they went to Mataria, a town a few miles north-west of present-day Cairo.

Whatever route they took to get there, it cannot have been too different from the road which Herod the king himself had taken in 42 BC when, having been deposed from his Tetrarchy by Antigonus, he fled to Alexandria to seek help from Antony.

Reckoning from Josephus's record of the route Herod took, we can reckon that Joseph and his family fled from Bethlehem over the western slopes of the mountains, towards Gaza. There they joined the road known as 'The Way of the Philistines,' that ran along the coast. In about three days, they reached Rhinocolura, the river of Egypt. Once on the south bank of the river – though it was really a wadi where water ran only after the winter rains – they were beyond Herod's reach.

They could breathe easily, now. And take the long rest they needed and deserved. And then continue their journey at a more leisurely pace, with time to dawdle sometimes.

Their route took them along the coast road, till they reached the sea-port of Pelusium. Then they bore south-west, along 'The Way of the Philistines,' till they came to Mataria, or On, as it is sometimes identified, or Heliopolis, on the banks of the Nile.

Mataria, On or Heliopolis was the city in which, tradition had it, that Moses was reared by Pharaoh's daughter. And it was at the university in On that the future deliverer of the Hebrews was educated in Egyptian theology, law and literature, and in the art of warfare. Moses became 'learned in all the wisdom of the Egyptians' (Acts 7:22). All of which, of course, equipped him for the task that still faced him – organising the Hebrews' exodus, and moving a nation of people to Canaan.

For Mary and Joseph, it was journey's end. The fleeing family had arrived.

Egypt was a natural choice as a place of refuge, for several good reasons, not the least of which was that the family could reach it quickly. While Joseph and his family would arrive as strangers, the could be sure of finding, in the Nile valley, a sizeable Jewish colony in which they could settle.

Egypt was, as this time, as it had been for almost two hundred years, flooded with Jews. They had been encouraged by the Ptolomies, and had prospered and increased under the favour shown to them. They'd had a temple in the Nile Delta for about one hundred years. They founded a new School of Jewish Theology, and had the Hebrew Bible translated into Greek – the Septuagint – for the benefit of non-Hebrews.

If the religious needs of Joseph's family were safely catered for, their domestic and economic needs were not neglected either.

In Egypt, Joseph would not have found it difficult to get work at his trade, or failing that, to find financial support. Jewish craftsmen in Egypt were formed into guilds – coppersmiths, goldsmiths, silversmiths, weavers, needle-makers, nail-makers … who supported members of their craft till they found work. Joseph was stonemason. And it's safe to assume that masons would support a brother mason.

At the same time, of course, the family had the security of the gold the Magi had brought as a gift. Despite the haste in escaping, it's unlikely Joseph would have left that behind in Bethlehem.

Egypt, however, was not without its snags.

For all the hundreds of Jews in Egypt, they were not the most loved people in the land. They were rivals in trade. They were favoured by the Romans. And this was enough to make the Greek merchants in Egypt, and the Egyptian people themselves, hate them. And the situation wasn't helped by the Jews themselves, who made no secret of the fact that they despised the Egyptian people for their heathenism.

But, for all that, Egypt provided Mary, Joseph and their child with a home, and a safe haven. Here they had arrived. And here they planned to stay till the same Providence which brought them here, would direct them to return to Judaea, to Bethlehem.

And that would be when Herod was dead. About three years after they'd first arrived in Egypt.

153-156In the meantime, though, the message which the angel had delivered to Joseph that Herod was 'going to seek the child to destroy him,' was fulfilled.

CHAPTER THIRTEEN

Murder
St Matthew 2:16-18

Then Herod,
seeing that he had been fooled by the Magi,
was furious,
and sent and killed all the boys in Bethlehem
and all its territory, who were two years old or under,
according to the time which he had learned from the Magi.

Then was fulfilled what was spoken through the
prophet Jeremiah, who said,

A voice was heard in Ramah,
wailing and great mourning,
Rachel weeping for her children,
and refusing to be comforted
because they were not.

It never crossed Herod's mind that the Magi would disobey him, any more than it entered the minds of the Magi to ignore the king's command.

Herod was not accustomed to having his commands ignored. And the Magi left their audience with the king on good terms and grateful for the full and generous information the king had given them. Herod, for long enough, had enough on his mind to distract him from thinking about the Magi and his request to them.

The king was a very sick man. His disease was slowly, and cruelly painfully killing him. The disease had set in some twenty-five years earlier, around the time he murdered Mariamne, the second of his ten wives. Her ghost still haunted him, even in the daytime.

Josephus, in his *Wars of the Jews*, describes the disease in every painful, stinking detail.

He writes: '... the distemper seized his whole body, and greatly disordered all its parts with various symptoms. There was a gentle fever on him, and an intolerable itching over all the surface of his body. And continual pains in his colon, and dropsical tumours about his feet. An inflamation of the abdomen, and a putrifaction of his privy member that produced worms. Besides which, he had a difficulty of breathing on him, and could not breathe but when he sat upright. And had a convulsion of all his members ...'

The description in his *Antiquities* is much the same, except that Josephus enlarges on a few of the details: '... a fire glowed in him slowly ... brought on him a vehement appetite for eating ... and aqueous and transparent liquor settled itself about his feet. A like matter afflicted him at the bottom of his belly ... He had difficulty in breathing, which was loathsome, on account of the stench of his breath and the quickness of its returns...'

Look at the Jewish historian's careful listing in the light of the information afforded by Rogers and Magaw in *Tropical Medicine*, and the impression is that Herod's terminal illness was schistosomiasis, also known as bilharzia.

The disease is caused by a parasite common in tropical countries, especially in Egypt, and the areas around Egypt.

Or to be precise, not to say pedantic, for a minute: the common parasite is called *Schistoma Haemotobium*. The parasite's invertebrate host is a small, freshwater snail. Schistosomiasis is caused by the Trematode worm of the family Schistosomidae. It enters the body in drinking water, or through the skin of people swimming or washing in infected waters.

There are several types of the disease. The most common in Egypt and the surrounding areas is either urinary or intestinal. The urinary disease is known to have been present in Egypt three thousand years ago. Eggs of the parasite have been found in mummies.

While the disease can attack anybody at any age, children

were most vulnerable, through bathing and paddling in infected waters. And there seems to have been no cure for the disease in Herod's day.

But the information in *Tropical Medicine* … Sir Leonard Rogers and Sir John Magaw list the symptoms in advanced cases of schistosomiasis: 'General urticaria with fever and abdominal pain. Urine is frequently passed, and the last portion contains blood. The urine may show white, threadlike pieces of mucus, or small blood clots. A large haemorrhage may be accompanied by the passge of worms. Sceptic infection may occur. The urethra may become thickened. Urinary Fistulas may result in the perineum or the penis itself, with great thickening of the organ, including the glans. Very great hard enlargement of the liver and spleen, producing a prominent abdomen. Fatal cirrhosis with ascites or oedema.'

Read Josephus's meticulous record against the background of this information, and Herod's awful condition is all too clear. The king had a massive infection of both urinary and intestinal origin. And it built up and worsened over the years.

Urticaria – commonly known as nettle rash – produced the 'gentle fever and intolerable itching all over the surface of his body.' Oedema – excess of water in the body – caused the king's 'dropsical tumours.' Worms produced his 'vehement appetite for eating.' Ascites – fluid in the abdomen – accounted for the 'aqueous and transparent liqour … at the bottom of his belly.'

Herod battled against his sickness. He battled to live, enduring unbearable agonies and pain, convincing himself that, in time, he would recover. Everything his physicians recommended, he did. Every potion and medicine they prescribed, he took.

This sick king, in a daily state of dying, waited for the Magi to bring him word of where the Messiah was to be found.

But, as yet, they had not come. Time passed. And still Herod waited. But still the Magi did not come. Until, at long last, Herod realised that the Magi were never coming back. They had made a fool of him. They mocked him.

And the sudden dawning of the truth, at the end of so long patience, drove him out of his mind.

'He was exceeding wroth,' as the Authorised Version has it or, as some modern versions have, 'He was furious,' hardly measures the state of Herod's mind.

St Matthew himself is careful in describing Herod's sudden reaction. And the word he uses is a rare word which appears nowhere else in the New Testament.

The word is *thumoo*. It means 'to be stirred up into a tumultuous state of mind'. It is an intense passion which may issue in anger or revenge. It is not the settled purpose of wrath (*orge*). It is the bursting out of the flame. Herod's mind was blown.

Josephus, when he writes of Herod's terminal illness, bears out the point St Matthew is making. 'Herod grew so choleric,' says Josephus, 'that it brought him to do things like a madman.' And it's this colour, this nuance in St Matthew's word, that has to affect the way we look at Herod's 'Massacre of the Innocents,' as his avenging act is known.

In a paroxysm of blind, raging madness, the king issues his order. None dare disobey. And the executioners are on their way to Bethlehem.

How easily the plan was mounted! How swiftly it was out into effect!

The executioners that were so easily and swiftly despatched to Bethlehem now, could just as easily have been sent when the Magi first made their enquiries. And, it was Herod himself who gained the information, and advised them of the whereabouts of the new-born Messiah.

Was his 'bring me word that I too may come and worship him,' genuine, after all?

The murdering Herod that could rid himself of the conspirators in the Pharisee Association in Jerusalem, and have his own sons murdered, did not kill Jochebed and her new-born son she claimed was the Messiah.

But, then, it was a calculating Herod. Then his mind was clear enough to plan. Now, however, it's a different Herod. This is Herod mad.

He 'sent and killed all the boys in Bethlehem and in all its territory, who were two years old and under, according to the time which he learned from the Magi.'

That any child at all was murdered is an unspeakable tragedy. At the same time, though, there's no value in exaggerating the number of the victims, as the Ethiopian legend certainly does, when it counts fourteen thousand. That's almost seven times the total population of Bethlehem at the time. Even if the villages of the hill country round Juttah are included – as the legend of Elizabeth fleeing with her infant, John, suggests – the number still cannot have been all that large.

According to St Matthew, Herod's order did not refer to 'all the children,' as some versions have it. It referred to 'all the boys,' (*pantas tous paidas*).

It may not have been more than twenty infant boys. It might have been ten.

The boys who were murdered were those, writes St Matthew, who were 'two years old and under, according to the time when he questioned the Magi.'

To come at what St Matthew means, it might be better to start at the end of his statement.

Herod calculated exactly when it was the Magi had come to him with their enquiries about the 'new-born king of the Jews.'

That boys up to two years old were to be murdered might suggest that Herod waited almost two years for the Magi to report back. Knowing what we know about Herod, that has to be highly unlikely. Even allowing that his sickness put the Magi out of his mind, it's still hard to believe that he could have forgotten for so long.

What St Matthew appears to be saying is that Herod reckoned that, at the time the Magi first arrived, the boy was either already born, or about to be born. One way or the other, then, he could now reckon that the child was still being suckled. Mothers in Israel suckled their sons for anything up to two years.

By killing the boys of 'two years old and under,' Herod was sure of hitting his intended target. And hit it, he most certainly did.

Tradition has it that the murdered infants were buried in or near Rachel's tomb, about ten minutes walk from Bethlehem.

St Matthew cannot hide his emotion as he feels the sorrow and pain that surrounded the burial, and the weeping and wailing of a town that followed the bereaved and broken-hearted parents in the funeral procession to Rachel's Tomb.

The Talmud quotes the Jewish legend about Rachel, and how she wept as all Israel was carried away captive to Babylon. 'When the children of Israel, laden with chains,' the Talmud says, 'were being driven off by the soldiers of Nebuchadnezzar into Babylon, the road led past the grave of our mother, Rachel. As they came near her grave, they heard cries of bitter weeping. It was the voice of Rachel, who had risen from her tomb, and was lamenting the fate of her unhappy children.'

St Matthew writes with sadness and tenderness, as though he trudged with those who travelled sorrow's bitter road.

Was the old legend in his mind, as he vented his own heartfelt emotion in a quotation that came to mind from Jeremiah, the weeping prophet?

'A voice was heard in Ramah, wailing and great mourning. Rachel weeping for her children, and refusing to be comforted because they were not.'

CHAPTER FOURTEEN

Return
St Matthew 2:19-23

On the death of Herod
the angel of the Lord appeared in a dream
to Joseph in Egypt,
saying, 'Get up, take the child and his mother,
and go into the land of Israel,
for they are dead who sought the child's life.'

He got up, took the child and his mother,
and went to the land of Israel.

When he heard that Archelaus
was king over Judaea in place of his father Herod
he was afraid to return there,
and being instructed in a dream
he withdrew to the region of Galilee.

He went and settled in a city called Nazareth,
that what was spoken through the prophets
might be fulfilled: 'He shall be called a Nazarene.'

'On the death of Herod.' The statement is simply written, and as quickly said. But, behind the sentence, hides a welter of events and emotions. A sick, warped, disillusioned man. A tyrant, still tyrannical till the day he died. A nation waiting to rejoice at his passing. His sons greedy to snatch the power their father's dying would bequeath to them.

Herod is now a man of about seventy years old. A desperately sick man, who felt himself despised and hated by the whole nation, and who convinced himself that the people rejoiced at his misfortunes.

As though his sickness were not already sufficient hardship
to contend with, Herod now had to deal with yet another plot
against his life. But this one devastated him. He might well wish
himself dead as the only way to be free of the unbearable pain
and degradation. He was not, however, prepared to allow himself to be killed. And certainly not by his own son. It's a long
story. It will make the telling that bit shorter, if we go into it
somewhere in the middle.

Pheroras, the king's brother, long ago put out of the palace, and
barred from any contact with the king, is living in Bethany-
beyond-Jordan. He's content, ruling his little principality of
Perea. And enjoying a good life with Jochebed, his wife, and
their young son who, to Jochebed's bitter disappointment,
turned out not to be the promised Messiah.

But now, Pheroras is sick, with a sudden sickness for which
his physicians can find no explanation. Nor can they find a cure.
Herod, in a surge of brotherly concern, visits Pheroras. The visit
could not have been more informal. No pomp, no royal en-
tourage. No more than a necessary few physicians and nursing
attendants. Herod the King is calling on his brother as a friend
might visit a neighbour.

The two sick brothers meet. And together weep.

And, still weeping, the king leaves.

And then Pheroras was dead.

Herod wept openly when he heard the news. The rumour in
the city was that the king had poisoned his brother. Herod ignored the rumours, and took no action against those who spread
them. He brought Pheroras to Jerusalem for burial. The king
himself arranged the funeral, with all the pomp and circumstance
of a prince's burial. And in the place of honour were Jochebed
and his brother's infant son.

It would be wise and right, he advised her, that she should
make her home in his palace in Jerusalem. And there the whole
matter might have rested, and been forgotten.

But two of Pheroras's freedmen made sure it should not be
forgotten.

When Pheroras's funeral was over, the two men came to Herod and pleaded with him to look into his brother's untimely death, and to avenge – what they considered to be – his murder.

Their plea, though they didn't realise it, was to start Herod on an enterprise which would uncover a cess-pit of hate, calumny and intrigue against himself. And lead, eventually, to the trial and death of his son Antipater.

Josephus reports the events in some detail in both his *Antiquities* and his *Wars of the Jews*.

As he says himself: 'I will explain the history of this matter distinctly, that it may be a warning for mankind, that they may take care of conducting their whole lives by the rules of virtue.'

The two men who made their plea to Herod were freedmen who were obviously long-standing servants to Pheroras, had served him well, and stood high in his esteem.

They brought the king hard facts. Pheroras and his wife, they assured the King, had eaten alone one evening, and during that meal, Jochebed had given her husband a potion in the food he was eating. After this, Pheroras had taken suddenly and inexplicably ill, and within days, he was dead. The king himself, they reminded Herod, had visited their master as he lay dying.

They also provided names. Jochebed's mother and her sister, Naomi had brought it to Jochebed the day before the supper. It was a love potion, they claimed. In reality, though, it was poison intended to kill Pheroras. It had come from Arabia. And they had got it from an intimate friend of one of Sylleus's mistresses. And, so far as they could make out, Antipater and his mother, Doris, were also involved.

Sylleus was a name already too familiar to Herod. The man was already in Rome awaiting trial before Caesar. And the charge was bribing Corinthus, one of Herod's own bodyguards, to kill the king. Antipater, the King's devoted son, had himself brought the man to Rome, on his way there to visit some old schoolboy friends, and make himself known to Caesar, in view of the fact that the king had nominated him as his heir and successor.

There were people to be punished. To decide what punishment, Herod would need some more evidence.

He began his search with the obvious people. The women's slave-girls were tortured. In his own bed chamber. In the bed chamber where he was dying a little more every day. The girls knew nothing. They admitted nothing. The torture was increased. Still they confessed nothing. One slave-girl, in the agonies of torture, cried out a prayer, 'May that God that governs the earth and the heaven, punish the author of all these our miseries, Antipater's mother.'

She told him nothing about the so-called love potion. But she talked about Antipater. His son had complained to Doris, his mother, that the king had lived too long ... The girl died as she spoke.

Herod now turned his attention to the men. And amongst them was one of Antipater's stewards. Ironically, the steward shared the same name.

It didn't take long to persuade him to talk. But there was no word from him about the love-potion that killed Pheroras. He talked, instead, about the poison which the king's son had provided to kill the king. Antiphilus, he explained, one of Antipater's friends, brought the poison from Egypt. He gave it to Theudion, brother of Doris, the mother of the king's son. Theudion sent it to Pheroras. And Pheroras gave it to his wife for safe keeping, till the opportunity should arise to kill the king.

Herod was hearing far more than he had bargained for. And he was to learn much more, and be told cruel truths when he examined Jochebed herself.

She answered the king's summons when he called her.

On his king's oath, he swore that, 'if she would speak the real truth, he would excuse her and all her servants from punishment.' But let her be warned. 'If she concealed anything, he would have her body torn to pieces by torments, and leave no part of it to be buried.'

'Upon this,' writes Josephus, with something of a sardonic touch, 'Upon this, the woman paused a little.' Of course she did.

Fear fired by imagination as she heard what Herod had in mind to do to her.

But she had lost none of her hate and spite and venom towards the king. One way or the other, she would die. The king wanted the truth. He would have the truth. This king who could outline his bestial cruelty in almost dulcet tones.

'Why do I spare to speak of these grand secrets, now that Pheroras is dead! That would only tend to save Antipater, who is all our destruction. Hear, then, O King, and be thou, and God himself, who cannot be deceived, witnesses to the truth of what I am going to say.'

And Herod heard every word she reported of Pheroras's dying confession, and his co-operation with Antipater to kill the king.

Herod could believe that. He had the measure of his brother. The man who could be persuaded by the king to arrange the murder of Alexander and Aristobulus, the king's sons, could as easily be encouraged to murder the king himself.

She was naming names he'd heard already – Antiphilus and his mother and brother, Theudion, her own mother and sister, Naomi.

But now she was adding new names. The king's wife, Mariamne, was amongst the conspirators. Mariamne's brothers. Mariamne's father, Simeon. And Simeon, the king didn't need to be reminded, was the High Priest. And did the king know that Bathyllus had just brought another poison – serpent venom – in case 'the first did not do the business'. Efficient Antipater had sent his no less efficient steward.

Jochebed was almost finished. She had given the king the truth he had demanded. She had concealed nothing.

Only one thing remained to be done. To give the king the phial of poison. She drew the box with its phial from her robes, and proferred it to the king. 'This I brought when my husband bade me, and emptied the greatest part of it into the fire, but reserved a little of it for my own use against uncertain futurity, and out of fear of thee.'

Herod had had more than enough of Jochebed. But he remembered his king's oath, and dismissed her.

It was not the end of the torturing, though.

Now came Antiphilus's mother and brother. Then Mariamne. And when her torturing brought her confession, Herod divorced her. Her brothers were next. And then Simeon, her father, the High Priest. When the king's father-in-law had been tortured enough, Herod took the High-priesthood away from him. 'And appointed Matthias the son of Theophilus, who was born at Jerusalem, to be high-priest in his room.'

Now the King must turn his mind to dealing with his son.

He wrote a letter to Antipater in Rome, requesting that he make no delay in coming home.

Came the day when Antipater arrived home from Rome, and already looking like a king. Bold, proud, and dressed in purple.

Fast messengers had brought the king word of his son's arrival by ship in Caesarea. He was already arranging the trial when Antipater appeared in the palace.

Quintilius Varus, the newly appointed President of Syria, was Herod's guest. It was a brief visit, Varus explained. He was on his way to Antioch to take up his appointment.

Herod understood, but wondered if Varus would agree to act as judge in his son's trial.

Varus would, of course. But he must be on his way to Antioch the day after tomorrow.

The trial, Herod assured him, would begin and end tomorrow.

Josephus writes up the episode in his *Wars of the Jews*, and his *Antiquities* . And, again, in great detail.

After seven months amongst the powerful people of Rome, and on the inner-fringe of Caesar's circle, could Antipater ever settle again in Judaea? He needn't have worried. If Antipater was disappointed when he stepped ashore at Caesarea, his treatment in the palace can only have filled him with a sense of doom and foreboding.

There was no fanfare welcome at the port. And nobody acknowledged him all along the road to Jerusaelm. Nobody dared. The king had ordered that his son be ignored. Besides which, the rumours about him were rife, and sufficiently derogatory to make him hated.

His father's greeting was, 'Vile wretch. May God confound you.' And then he went on bluntly to explain that tomorrow he would be tried in court. The charge was parricide. And Quintillius Varus would preside as judge.

The Court assembled next day.

The trial was brief, bitter and acrimonious.

The Court had hardly come to order before Antipater fell on his face in front of his father, beseeching him not to prejudge the case. 'Father, I beseech you, do not condemn me beforehand, but let your ears be unbiassed, and attend to my defence. If you will give me leave, I will demonstrate that I am innocent.'

The King cut him off. But addressed his remarks to Varus, the judge. 'I cannot but think,' he said, 'that you, and every other upright judge, will determine that Antipater is a vile wretch.'

Antipater, he explained, was marked to be his successor. But the king was living too long. And Antipater could not wait, 'but would be a king by parricide.' And this parricide would presume to speak for himself! 'You must guard yourself against him, Varus. I know the wild beast. And I foresee how plausibly he will talk, and his counterfeit lamentation.'

This man, he pointed out, took care of my sleep, he was my protector, the guardian of my body. 'I can hardly believe I am still alive.'

Herod had one more thing to say. 'I am resolved that no one who thirsts for my blood shall escape punishment, although the evidence should extend to all my sons.'

Herod stopped. Sat down. And wept.

Antipater heard the sobbing, and looked up. He could see Nicolaus of Damascus rising, at the king's signal, to begin the prosecution.

He took advantage of the lull before Nicolaus began. Still prostrate, he called out, 'My Father, you have yourself made my apology for me. How can I be a parricide whom you declare was always your guardian?'

Antipater had the Court's attention.

'You call my filial affection prodigious lies and hypocrisy ...' As he spoke, he reached into his robes, and pulled out a package of letters. 'Rome is a witness to my filial affection,' he declared. 'And so is Caesar, the ruler of the habitable earth. He called me Philopater – a lover of his father.' He raised himself up, reaching out the letters. 'Take these letters which Caesar has sent. They are more to be believed than the calumnies raised here. These letters are my only apology.'

And now he spoke softly, watching the response of sympathy grow in Varus's face. 'If I am to be condemned, I beg that you will not believe those who have been tortured. If I be a parricide, let fire be brought to torment me. Let the racks pass through my bowels. Have no regard to any lamentation that this polluted body can make. If I be a parricide, I ought not to die without torture.'

Antipater broke down in tears. And lay convulsed in sobbing and lamentation.

And, as Josephus reports, 'Moved all the rest, and Varus in particular, to commiserate his case.'

The hearing might have ended there, and Varus might have ruled in Antipater's favour. But Nicolaus rose. The prosecution, he pointed out, had been interrupted by Antipater. It still had to present its case.

Nicolaus was neat, efficient. And scathing.

He could not, he explained, but stand amazed at Antipater's horrid wickedness. 'Although this man has had great benefits bestowed on him by his father ... enough to tame his reason,' he told the Court, 'Yet this man could no more be tamed than the most envenomed serpent. Even those creatures,' he reminded them, 'admit to some mitigation, and will not bite their benefactors. But Antipater ...'

He turned to look at the figure on the floor, still prostrate like a suppliant.

Every damning word he spoke now, was addressed directly at Antipater, as he outlined the case against him in every sordid detail. If those in the Court were ignorant and unaware of Antipater's crimes before the trial had begun, they were left in no doubt by the time Nicolaus had finished.

'You would kill your father. And devised such a sort of uncommon parricide as the world never yet saw. And you did it while he loved you, and was your benefactor.'

The Court could measure what he'd said as he paused long enough to take a deep breath.

His voice had its own touch of venom as he leaned towards Antipater. 'You have a mind more cruel than any serpent.' And then, like a snake that would kill its prey, he lashed, 'And from that mind, you sent out poison. Against an old man.'

He still had more venom left. 'You allege that those who were tortured told lies, that those who were the deliverers of your father must not be considered as having told the truth, But ...' and Nicolaus almost whispered his sarcasm, 'but your own tortures may be esteemed discoverers of the truth!'

He stopped, stood straight, and addressed himself, now, to the judge. 'Will you not, Varus, deliver the king of the injuries of his kin? Will you not destroy this wicked wild beast who appears to be the bloddiest butcher of them all?'

It was a good note on which to end his speech. There was, though, an important note to add. Varus and the Court had been prepared to be swayed by Antipater's earlier act. It must not happen again. He was here as Herod's friend. And, for his sake, Antipater must die.

Nicolaus would never presume to teach the newly appointed President of Syria in the law. But, as the prosecutor in this case, he must, at least, remind the judge of the enormity of the crime of which Antipater stood accused. 'You are aware, Varus,' he addressed the judge, 'that parricide is a general injury both to nature, and to comman life.'

The judge knew.

'The intention of parricide,' the prosecutor pointed out, 'is not inferior to its preparation. And he who does not punish it, is injurious to nature itself.'

Nicolaus had no more to say.

Varus asked if Antipater had anything to say in his own defence.

Antipater lay long in silence. And when he spoke, 'God is my witness that I am entirely innocent,' was all he said.

Varus pronounced him guilty, and ordered that he be imprisoned in chains, to await Caesar's advice as to whether he should be killed or not.

The Court rose.

Next day, as he had planned, Varus left Jerusalem to take up his new post in Antioch.

They brought the King to Jericho. Being in the city he loved, might have brightened his spirit. It did nothing, however, to improve his health. His condition worsened. He was in constant, unremitting pain. Every inch of his body itched. Breathing was hard enough when he was propped, and sitting upright. It was almost impossible lying down. His stench disgusted even himself. Useless as the situation was , Herod struggled to live. And constantly hoped for recovery.

For all his physicians' concern, they felt themselves becoming more and more useless. They made concoctions, and the king swallowed them. They recommended treatments, and he docilely bore them. Whatever medicine they prescribed, he took.

The king readily agreed with the physicians' suggestion that he should go to Callirrhoe. There were hot baths there whose waters ran into the Dead Sea – or Lake Asphaltitis, as Josephus calls it. The asphaltic waters were said to have curative properties, and were sweet to drink.

Buoyed up with hope, Herod travelled, across the Jurdan, to the east side of the Dead Sea, to Callirrhoe. He allowed himself to be bathed again and again in the curative waters. And gluttonously swallowed large doses of the water.

To no avail.

Would bathing in warm oil cure the king, they wondered.

The king didn't know, but listened to their reason. A disease which had been contracted through the skin, might well be curable with medication through the skin. They agreed it was a dangerous move. But it was worth a try. They knew … even the king knew … that left as he was the king would die anyway.

So, they bathed him in hot oil.

Whatever the hot oil did by way of pain and blistering and agony, and very nearly killing him, it did nothing at all to improve the disease that tormented him.

They brought him back to Jericho.

Herod spent his days hovering between the wish to die and the obstinate will to live just long enough to see his son Antipater punished.

Whatever he lacked in good health, however, he made up for in villainy.

Admittedly, as Josephus reports, 'he grew so choleric that it brought him to do things like a madman.' It was still a hardship for those on the receiving end of his madness.

He commanded that, 'all the principal men of the entire Jewish nation, wheresoever the lived, should be called to him.'

And the principal men came in their droves. They had, of course, no alternative. 'Death was the penalty of such as should despise the epistles that were sent to them.'

There's no way of knowing exactly what the king had in mind when he first issued the order. What happened when they arrived in Jericho was that Herod 'developed a sudden wild rage against them all'. He ordered that they all be shut up in the Hippodrome he had built when he built the city. It was a place for chariot and horse-racing.

Now, he summoned his sister Salome, and her husband, Alexas.

Josephus reports in full what Herod said to them: 'I know well enough that the Jews will keep a festival upon my death. However, it is in my power to be mourned for on other accounts, and to have a splendid funeral, if you will but be subservient to my commands. Do you but take care to send soldiers to encompass these men that are now in custody, and slay them immediately upon my death. And then, all Judaea, and every family of them will weep at it whether they will or no.'

He was a bit brighter for the next few days. Largely because of the news from Rome. Caesar approved the sentence passed on Antipater, and condemned him to die. However, Caesar left it to Herod 'to act as became a father and a king, and either to banish him or take away his life, which he pleased.'

But his disease and its attendant miseries came, rampaging back. He couldn't breathe. He had a convulsive cough. And a voracious appetite that clamoured to be satisfied.

He took an apple from the dish on his bedside table. And asked for a knife to pare it.

He looked around to make sure there was nobody about who might stop him. And he lifted his right hand to stab himself, and end it all.

His first cousin, Achiabus, however, saw him, roared out, raced to him, and grabbed his hand.

Achiabus's cry rang through the palace, and everybody in the palace decided the king was dead.

In next to no time, the news reached Antipater, in prison.

Antipater decided that the king must, indeed, be dead. Now, he would be released from his chains, and from prison, and would take over the kingdom.

He talked to the jailer, told him to release him, and promised all kinds of rewards.

The jailer, however, went and informed the king.

Herod, at death's door, raved like a lunatic, roaring and banging his head. He lifted himself up on his elbow, summoned his guards, and commanded them to kill Antipater immediately. 'And bury him in a ignoble manner at Hyrcania.'

Then, the King changed his will. Antipas, whom he once named as his successor, was now named as Tetrarch of Galilee. Philip was named Tetrarch of Gaulonitis, Trachonitis and Paneas. Archelaus was named to succeed him as king.

Part of his kingdom he bequeathed to Salome, with five hundred thousand silver coins. The will provided rich bequests for all his relatives. To Caesar he bequeathed ten million drachmae. And garments of rich cloth to Caesar's wife, Julia.

A few days later, the King was dead.

It was said of Herod that 'He slunk to the throne like a fox, he reigned like a tiger, and died like a dog.'

Salome and Alexas decided to keep Herod's death a secret until they had released the 'principal men,' imprisoned and awaiting death in the Hippodrome. The reason for their release, she eplained to them, was that the king had changed his mind. His order, now, was that they go back to their own places, and take care of their own affairs.

Next, she summoned the whole population and the army to attend in the amphitheatre in Jericho.

The noise and confusion of people crowding, raucous and boiterous, tier on tier, sounded all over Jericho. It seemed like a public holiday. The army added its own clamour to the cauldron of pandemonium.

Trumpets blasting sounded silence for the start. Salome announced to them all that the king was dead. They all knew already. But they had to be informed officially.

She read to the soldiers the letter Herod had left, addressed to them. In it, he thanked them for their fidelity and their goodwill to himself. He exhorted them to afford the same loyalty and devotion to their new king.

The soldiers cheered. And they meant it. Herod himself meant it. He loved his soldiers, their roughness and bravery, and often revelled in their roistering.

Ptolemy, the Keeper of the King's Seal, followed Salome, and proclaimed the succession.

The proclamation was a little premature, if not, indeed, presumptuous. The appointments and nominations in Herod's will still needed approval and ratification by the Emperor, Augustus Caesar.

The amphitheatre resounded with the people's acclamation of their new king shouting, clapping, roaring, stamping, pounding. Whether or not they meant it, didn't matter. It was their duty.

And Archelaus, already dressed, and looking like a king, received the plaudits. And from the king's box, watched as the soldiers marched and counter-marched, proud and powerful, troop by troop and band by band, to swear allegiance and fidelity and their readiness to serve him. 'And they prayed God to be assistant to him.'

Archelaus's first task as king was to arrange his father's funeral. And this, he decided, would be the most splendid thing the country had ever seen. If Herod died like a dog, Archelaus saw to it that he was buried like an emperor.

The body of the dead king was carried on a golden bier, embroidered with precious stones. It was draped with purple. The dead king himself was covered with purple. He had a diadem on his head and, above it, a crown of gold, and a sceptre in his right hand. His sons and all his relatives were ranged around the bier. Next to these, the army, 'distinguished,' as the historian reports, 'according to their several countries and denominations. These were followed by five hundred of his domestics, carrying spices.'

They moved out. And marched eight furlongs a day. Which means, in fact, that Herod's funeral procession took no less than twenty-five days.

So, the King was buried.

Herod's thirty-seven years reign was ended.

St Matthew sums it all up in what must be the shortest shorthand note on any piece of history – 'Now when Herod was dead.'

'In Egypt,' he goes on to write, 'the angel of the Lord appeared in a dream to Joseph, saying, "Get up, take the child and his mother, and go into the land of Israel, for they are dead who sought the child's life".'

Obedient as ever to the divine command, Joseph took his wife and the child, and set-off on their journey home.

How long were they in Egypt? It's generally accepted that Jesus was born in 7 BC. Herod died in 4 BC. An easy sum in subtraction, gives the number of years. The Holy Family were three years in Egypt. Jesus, then, was about three years of age when the family began their journey.

Now they travelled, in the reverse direction, the same road along which they had sped in their flight from Herod's threat.

From Mataria to Pelusium, across the wadi Rhinoncolura, along the 'Way of the Philistines' that skirted the coast, to Gaza, 'and came into the Land of Israel.'

The instruction to Joseph in his dream, was that he should 'go into the land of Israel.'

That Joseph understood this to mean that he should return to Bethlehem in Judaea, is clear from St Matthew's record. The change of plan was forced on Joseph when he learnt that Bethlehem, like the rest of Judaea, was now under the rule of Archelaus.

St Matthew gives the feel of the dilemma that faced Joseph. 'When he heard that Archelaus was king over Judaea in place of his father Herod, he was afraid to return there. And being instructed in a dream, he withdrew to the region of Galilee.'

It was clearly in Joseph's mind to go back to Bethlehem. But he is afraid of the consequences of going back to Bethlehem, yet feels himself bound to obey the instructions in the dream that made him leave Egypt in the first place.

The wording of the command, though, is broad enough to allow Joseph, at the end of his struggle within himself, to solve his problem.

He followed the instructions by coming 'into the land of Israel'. But, taking the instructions of his second dream, he steers clear of whatever danger might lurk in Bethlehem, by not heading for the town when the family crossed the border of Egypt and Israel.

It's almost inevitable that they should choose a place with which they were already familiar. Despite the reasons which drove them out a few years earlier. They continued their journey by the coast road, towards Galilee and Nazareth.

St Matthew's note that 'Archelaus was king over Judaea,' combined with the fact that Joseph could feel he would be safe in Galilee, hints that Joseph and his family arrived back in Israel when the squabble bewteen Antipas and Archelaus for succession was ended, and finally settled in Rome by Caesar.

Neither of them was made king. Instead, Caesar ignored the details and nominations in Herod's will. He divided the kingdom between the three brothers, Antipas, Philip, and Archelaus. The Emperor's promise to Archelaus was that, if he ruled Judaea well as Ethnarch, then he would later confer on him the royal dignity.

But Archelaus was no ruler. And he proved it from the day he first assumed his right to the kingdom. He has barely begun ruling before Judaea is in chaos. Josephus paints the picture of the hopeless state of affairs under Archelaus: 'Now at this time there were ten thousand other disorders in Judaea ...' Even two thousand of Herod's old soldiers who had been disbanded, formed themselves into a regiment, and fought the troops of Archelaus in Judaea.

Joseph, then, had no need to have his ear close to the ground to hear what was happening in the region. The noise of it was all around him. And, while Galilee, under Antipas, was suffering its own upheavals, at least it was safer ground than that in Archelaus's jurisdiction.

So, instead of going to Bethlehem, they went to Mary's home-town, Nazareth.

St Matthew and St Luke each has his own way of concluding his account of the birth of Jesus.

St Matthew ends his account in a 'full-stop' kind of way. 'He went and settled in a city called Nazareth.'

St Luke, though, gives the feeling that he's merely 'rounding-off,' what is really only the introduction to the whole story: '... they returned to Galilee, to their city, Nazareth.'

He may be short-circuiting history, but he adds a gentle, appealing touch. 'The child grew, and became strong, being filled with wisdom.' And then, the lovely closing line, 'And the grace of God was upon him.'

It's a storyteller's ending. It hints that there's more to come. His readers can expect a sequel.